HISTORY OF IMMIGRATION

TO THE

UNITED STATES,

EXHIBITING THE

NUMBER, SEX, AGE, OCCUPATION, AND COUNTRY OF BIRTH,

OF

PASSENGERS ARRIVING IN THE UNITED STATES

BY SEA FROM FOREIGN COUNTRIES, FROM SEPTEMBER 30, 1819, TO DECEMBER 31, 1855;

COMPILED ENTIRELY FROM OFFICIAL DATA:

WITH

AN INTRODUCTORY REVIEW OF THE PROGRESS AND EXTENT OF IMMIGRATION TO THE UNITED STATES PRIOR TO 1819,

AND AN APPENDIX CONTAINING THE

NATURALIZATION AND PASSENGER LAWS

OF THE UNITED STATES, AND EXTRACTS FROM THE LAWS OF THE SEVERAL STATES RELATIVE TO IMMIGRANTS, THE IMPORTATION OF PAUPERS, CONVICTS, LUNATICS, ETC.

By WILLIAM J. BROMWELL,
OF THE DEPARTMENT OF STATE.

REDFIELD,
34 BEEKMAN STREET, NEW YORK.
1856.

SAVAGE & McCREA, STEREOTYPERS,
13 Chambers Street, N. Y.

PREFACE.

To the citizens of the United States the following History of Immigration is respectfully submitted, in the belief that it will prove to them an acceptable offering, since, by the aid of the facts contained therein, they may accurately determine the elements which have contributed to the unexampled growth of the American Republic.

As to the question of the good or bad effect resulting to this country from immigration, the author earnestly disclaims the desire to promulgate any opinion which he may entertain; he has, in the compilation of this history, embodied *facts only:* and, he leaves it to the enlightened understanding of the people of the United States to arrive at just conclusions from the premises therein presented.

The Statements contained in it have been compiled, entirely, from official documents:—

First, and chiefly, from the Annual Reports on Immigration prepared at the Department of State, and by the Secretary communicated to Congress in compliance with a requirement of the Passenger Act of March 2, 1819.

Secondly, from Passenger Abstracts transmitted to the Secretary of State by Collectors of the Customs, and on file in the Department, yet not embraced in the Annual Reports on Immigration, because not received until those Reports had been completed and laid before Congress.

Thirdly, from such custom-house records as furnished immigration statistics never communicated to the Secretary, or which, if ever communicated, are now missing from the files of the Department.

The facts thus accumulated, and exhibited in the tables which follow, contain all the available official information of importance in possession of the country relative to its immigration.

Fifteen months have elapsed since the compilation of this work was begun, and almost every hour not employed in the discharge of official duties has been devoted to the task. Even a cursory examination of the published Reports on Immigration, to be found in the Executive Documents of Congress, will show the extent and intricacy of the author's labors. The first Report, embracing returns for the year ending September 30, 1820, consists of literal copies of passenger manifests containing over ten thousand names, to each of which are affixed the corresponding age, sex, occupation, and country of birth; thus presenting in detail, and without classification, more than fifty thousand items, forming a book of about three hundred pages. In the present work, recapitulations of that Report are given, occupying only four pages.

The subsequent Reports, although more condensed than the one mentioned, are quite voluminous. Many of them are without method, have no recapitulations appended to them, and, as published, contain numerous typographical as well as clerical errors. Even the Reports for the last three years, which have been prepared with great care, and which are much more perfect than those preceding, have been recapitulated anew in order to embrace additional information, and to secure a systematic classification.

In conclusion, the author remarks, that, from the commencement of this work to the completion of it, he has been mindful of the fact, that, to the general reader it can not prove attractive; and the only encouragement he has received to prosecute the task and to finish it, has been derived from the consideration that a history of Immigration, exhibiting the *number and sex*, *age*, *occupation*, and *country of birth*, of passengers arriving in the United States, so far as the same is officially known, would, if presented to the public in the present form, never become obsolete, nor be supplanted by another work of a similar kind, but would exist as a book of reference so long as the American People shall feel an interest in a subject which so vitally concerns them.

WASHINGTON, D. C., *March*, 1856.

INTRODUCTORY REMARKS.

PROGRESS AND EXTENT OF IMMIGRATION PRIOR TO 1819.

We will first consider very briefly the progress and extent of immigration to the United States of America prior to 1819, the year in which the present official history begins. As, on this point, no authentic information exists, it must be determined by such evidence as statisticians of that period possessed, and by the relations then existing between the United States and the countries from which persons emigrated.

The current of migration commenced its flow from England, Ireland, and Scotland, and from Germany through the French and British ports. It was subject to many fluctuations during a part of this time, but continued with considerable uniformity, it is believed, until 1806.

Mr. Samuel Blodget, a statistician of more than ordinary research and accuracy, wrote in 1806, while every fact in regard to immigration was fresh in the minds of the people, that from "the best records and estimates at present attainable," the immigrants arriving in this country did not average, for the ten years from 1784 to 1794, more than 4,000 per annum.*

During 1794, 10,000 persons were estimated to have arrived in the United States from foreign countries.†

In 1818, Dr. Adam Seybert, member of the House of Represen

* Blodget's Statistical Manual, page 75.

† Cooper's Information respecting America. London, 1795.

tatives from Pennsylvania, in his exceedingly valuable "Statistical Annals" of the United States, wrote to the following effect:—

"Though we admit that ten thousand foreigners may have arrived in the United States in 1794, we can not allow that they did so, in an equal number, in any preceding or subsequent year, until 1817;" and he assumes that 6,000 persons arrived in the United States from foreign countries in each year from 1790 to 1810:* to him, and to the authorities he consulted, this average seemed a generous one.

During the ten years from 1806 to 1816, extensive immigration to the United States was precluded by the unfriendly relations at that time existing between Great Britain, France, and the United States.

England maintained the doctrine, and for a while enforced it with success, that "a man, once a subject, was always a subject." This deterred many from emigrating to this country from the British empire. Numbers had previously come for the purpose of entering the American merchant-service, and numbers still might have come which the fear of British impressment frightened from carrying out their design.

Another influence retarded immigration: in 1806, Great Britain issued a decree declaring the coasts of France in a state of blockade. A retaliatory decree was, in November of the same year, issued by France, declaring the British isles in a state of blockade.

To these restrictions on commerce—and, consequently, on the unobstructed passage from Europe—succeeded the British orders in council, and the Milan decree of Napoleon.

In March, 1809, the United States law was passed prohibiting for one year intercourse with Great Britain and France.

In 1810, the Napoleonic decrees were annulled; and the commerce of the United States had, in 1811, fairly commenced with France, but only to have their vessels fall into the hands of the British.

Preparations were now making for active hostilities, and on the

* Seybert's Annals, pp. 28 and 29.

18th of June, 1812, war was formally declared by the United States to exist with Great Britain.

The German emigration sensibly felt this unfavorable condition of affairs, inasmuch as the Germans embarked principally at the ports of Liverpool and Havre; facilities for migrating thence to this country being more numerous, and the expense of the voyage less onerous. Thus, from 1806, was the stream of emigration pent up at its fountain.

In February, 1815, peace was concluded between the United States and Great Britain; and, after several months requisite to restore tranquillity and to secure the confidence of those desiring to leave the Old World, the tide resumed its flow,* and with a speed greatly accelerated: as, from authentic information, collected principally at the several customhouses, it appears that, during the year 1817, not less than 22,240 persons arrived at ports of the United States from foreign countries. This number included American citizens returning from abroad.†

In no year previous to that had one half so many foreign passengers reached our shores. Many sufferings were incident to a voyage across the Atlantic in a crowded emigrant-vessel; and there were no laws of the United States either limiting the number of persons which a passenger ship or vessel should be entitled to carry, or providing any measures for the health or accommodation of the passengers. The subject seemed to deserve the immediate attention of Congress. In 1818 (March 10), Louis M'Lane, of Delaware, reported to the House of Representatives a bill "regulating passenger ships and vessels," which was read twice and referred.‡

In December of the following session it was called up by Thomas Newton, of Virginia, who explained the necessity of its passage. It was read a third time and passed by the House.

* Even in 1816 emigration was to some extent impeded. An act of the British Parliament allowed vessels to carry from Great Britain and Ireland to the United States only one passenger for every five tons, while it allowed vessels to carry to other foreign countries one passenger for every two tons.

† Seybert, p. 29.

‡ See Annals of Congress, 1818 and 1819.

After receiving amendments from both the Senate and House, it was finally passed, and approved March 2, 1819.*

In compliance with a requirement of this act, collectors of the customs have reported quarter-yearly to the Secretary of State the number of passengers arriving in their collection-districts by sea from foreign countries; also the sex, age, and occupation, of such passengers, and the country in which they were born. Annual reports, embracing that information, have, in conformity with the same act, been communicated to Congress by the Secretary of State; and, as before indicated, from these reports, chiefly, this history has been compiled.

The following statement† exhibits the

PROGRESS AND EXTENT OF IMMIGRATION TO THE UNITED STATES, FROM SEPTEMBER 30, 1819, TO DECEMBER 31, 1855.

PERIOD OF YEARS.	Total Number of Passengers arriving.	Of Foreign Birth.
During the 10 years ending Sept. 30, 1829	151,636	128,502
" " 10¼ " " Dec. 31, 1839	572,716	538,381
" " 9¾ " " Sept. 30, 1849	1,479,478	1,427,337
" " 6¼ " " Dec. 31, 1855	2,279,007	2,118,404
" " 36¼ " " " " "	4,482,837	4,212,624

Of the 4,212,624 passengers of foreign birth arriving in the United States during the above-mentioned period of 36¼ years—

207,492 were born in England;
747,930 " " " Ireland;
34,559 " " " Scotland;
4,782 " " " Wales; and—
1,348,682 others were born in Great Britain and Ireland, the division not designated.
―――――
2,343,445 total number born in the United Kingdom.

* For this and all other passenger-acts of the United States, see APPENDIX.

† Instead of this, any other combination of years may readily be adopted, the comparative statements (pp. 174 and 175) having been so prepared as to afford every facility for that purpose.

.,206,087 were born in Germany;
35,995 " " " Prussia;
17,583 " " " Holland;
6,991 " " " Belgium;
31,071 " " " Switzerland;
188,725 " " " France;
11,251 " " " Spain;
6,049 " " " Portugal;
3,059 " " " Denmark;
29,441 " " " Norway and Sweden;
1,318 " " " Poland;
938 " " " Russia;
123 " " " Turkey;
7,185 " " " Italy;
108 " " " Greece;
338 " " " Sicily;
706 " " " Sardinia;
9 " " " Corsica;
116 " " " Malta;
526 others were born in Europe, the division not designated.

91,699 were born in British America;
5,440 " " " South America;
640 " " " Central America;
15,969 " " " Mexico;
35,317 " " " the West Indies.

16,714 were born in China;
101 " " " the East Indies;
7 " " " Persia;
16 others were born in Asia, division not designated.

14 were born in Liberia;
4 " " " Egypt;
5 " " " Morocco;
2 " " " Algiers;
4 others were born in the Barbary States, the division not designated.
2 were born at the Cape of Good Hope.
118 others were born in Africa, the division not designated.

278	were	born	at	the	Canary Islands;	
1,288	"	"	"	"	Azore	"
203	"	"	"	"	Madeira	"
22	"	"	"	"	Cape Verde	
59	"	"	"	"	Sandwich	"
5	"	"	"	"	Society	"
79	"	"	"	"	South Sea	"
3	"	"	"	"	Isle of France;	
14	"	"	"		St. Helena;	
20	"	"	"		Australia; and—	

157,537 others were born in countries not designated in the returns made by collectors of the customs.

The country having the largest emigration is, doubtless, Ireland; for, in addition to the 747,930 persons arriving from the United Kingdom, known to have been born in Ireland, it is safe to assume that, of the 1,348,682 others born, as indefinitely stated, in "Great Britain and Ireland," arriving in the United States, 1,000,000 were born in Ireland alone, thus making 1,747,930 as the total Irish emigration.

Next in numerical order comes Germany; England, third; and France, fourth.

The emigration of Chinese to this country was very inconsiderable until 1854, previous to which year the aggregate number known to have arrived was only 88. In that year, however, 13,100 came to the United States; and, in 1855, 3,526; all of whom, with the exception of a single passenger, landed at the port of San Francisco: 15,950 were males, and were designated in the returns of the collector as "Laborers."

As regards passengers from British America, the fact may be deemed worthy of mention, that many of them, especially of those arriving during the last four years, are known to have come with the intention of returning, and not of residing in the United States. The number of such can not, however, be determined.

Finally, to the 4,212,624 passengers of foreign birth arriving in the United States since September 30, 1819, may be added 250,000 as the number of immigrants who arrived prior to that date; making the total of foreign arrivals from the close of the Revolutionary War to December 31, 1855, 4,462,624.

LEGAL RIGHTS OF NATURALIZED CITIZENS.

ALIENS, naturalized agreeably to the acts of Congress,* are not prohibited by the constitution of the United States the enjoyment of the same rights, and to the same extent, as natural-born citizens—with the single proviso that no person shall be eligible to the office of President or Vice-President except a citizen native born, or a citizen of the United States at the time of the adoption of the federal constitution:

Congress can make no law to prohibit the free exercise of their religion; nor to abridge their freedom of speech:

The right of security in their persons, houses, papers, and effects, against unreasonable searches and seizures, is not denied to them; nor are they prohibited the purchase and occupation of lands owned by the government.

The constitutions of the several states concede to naturalized citizens, who may take up their residence within the states, in general the same rights as are enjoyed by persons born therein. Among these rights may be mentioned that of electing and of being elected to office.

* See Appendix.

PLAN OF THE WORK.

Not only may the *extent* of each year's immigration to the United States be learned from the statements contained in this work, but also the *character* of that immigration. These statements exhibit—

I.—Arrivals—Number and Sex.
II.—Age.
III.—Occupation.
IV.—Country where born.

In the Appendix will be found extracts from the laws of the several states relative to immigrants, the importation of paupers, convicts, lunatics, &c.

EXPLANATION OF TERMS USED IN THE WORK.

Under the head of Occupation, occur the following terms:—

Other occupations—comprising such occupations as are not otherwise recapitulated in the statement; chiefly soldiers, civil and military officers, &c., and in general those occupations to which belonged so small a number as to require no special designation.

Not stated—Males. These were returned by collectors of the customs as having no occupation, and comprise for the greater part those under fifteen years of age.

Under the head of Country where born occur the following terms:—

Great Britain and Ireland—Comprising those born in the United Kingdom, and not included in either "England," "Ireland," "Scotland," or "Wales"—returned thus indefinitely by collectors of the customs.

Europe......
Asia........
Barbary States
Africa......
} The division not designated.

Statements exhibiting the *Number and Sex*, *Age*, *Occupation*, and *Country of Birth*, of Passengers arriving in the United States by sea from foreign countries during the year ending September 30, 1820.

I.—ARRIVALS.—Number and Sex.

PORTS AT WHICH THEY ARRIVED.		Males.	Females.	Sex not stated.	Total.
Portland and Falmouth	Me.	99	38	...	137
Belfast	"	71	26	29	126
Waldoboro'	"	3	3	...	6
Kennebunk	"	3	...	...	3
Wiscasset	"	3	...	...	3
Portsmouth	N. H.	6	1	4	11
Boston and Charlestown	Mass.	636	172	53	861
Edgartown	"	42	18	...	60
Dighton	"	12	...	...	12
Nantucket	"	3	...	...	3
Marblehead	"	2	...	...	2
Barnstable	"	3	3	...	6
Newport	R. I.	24	15	...	39
Providence	"	7	...	...	7
Bristol	"	24	...	...	24
New London	Ct.	7	...	...	7
New Haven	"	6	...	...	6
Fairfield	"	2	...	...	2
New York City	N. Y.	2233	992	609	3834
Wilmington	Del.	7	3	...	10
Philadelphia	Pa.	1102	621	327	2050
Baltimore	Md.	842	394	26	1262
Georgetown	D. C.	15	9	...	24
Alexandria	"	6	...	...	6
Norfolk and Portsmouth	Va.	106	43	15	164
Richmond	"	43	32	...	75
Petersburg	"	11	12	4	27
Plymouth	N. C.	6	...	...	6
Edenton	"	102	18	3	123
Newbern	"	19	...	...	19
Charleston	S. C.	296	82	7	385
Savannah	Ga.	68	14	4	86
New Orleans	La.	624	184	103	911
Sandusky	Ohio	14	...	...	14
Total		6447	2680	1184	10311

II.—AGE.

AGES.	Males.	Females.	Sex not stated.	Total.
Under 5 years of age . . .	241	188	. . .	429
Between 5 years of age and 10 .	226	196	. . .	422
Between 10 years of age and 15 .	247	213	2	462
Between 15 years of age and 20 .	485	289	. . .	774
Between 20 years of age and 25 .	1346	446	. . .	1792
Between 25 years of age and 30 .	1207	395	2	1604
Between 30 years of age and 35 .	829	271	. . .	1100
Between 35 years of age and 40 .	590	201	3	794
40 years of age and upward . .	1104	412	2	1518
Age not stated	172	69	1175	1416
Total . . .	6447	2680	1184	10311

III.—OCCUPATION.

OCCUPATIONS.	Males.	Fe-males.	Sex not stated.	Total.
Merchants	933	...	...	933
Farmers	874	...	...	874
Mechanics	269	...	...	269
Mariners	336	...	...	336
Miners	4	...	...	4
Laborers	334	...	...	334
Shoemakers	62	...	...	62
Tailors	63	...	...	63
Seamstresses and Milliners	...	35	...	35
Actors	2	...	...	2
Weavers and Spinners	85	5	...	90
Clergymen	24	...	...	24
Clerks	63	...	...	63
Lawyers	6	...	...	6
Physicians	43	...	...	43
Engineers	12	...	...	12
Artists	9	...	...	9
Teachers	17	2	...	19
Musicians	2	...	...	2
Printers	5	...	...	5
Painters	17	...	...	17
Masons	27	...	...	27
Hatters	5	...	...	5
Manufacturers	13	...	...	13
Millers	7	...	...	7
Butchers	36	...	...	36
Bakers	46	...	...	46
Servants	66	72	1	139
Other occupations	328	9	...	337
Not stated	2759	2557	1183	6499
Total	6447	2680	1184	10311

IV.—COUNTRY WHERE BORN.

COUNTRIES.	Males.	Females.	Sex not stated.	Total.
England	967	561	254	1782
Ireland	944	572	209	1725
Scotland	173	75	20	268
Great Britain and Ireland	1179	640	430	2249
British America	134	64	11	209
France	282	58	31	371
Spain	133	4	2	139
Portugal	30	5	...	35
Italy	19	4	2	25
Turkey	1	...	...	1
Sardinia	3	2	...	5
Switzerland	24	6	1	31
Belgium	1	...	...	1
Holland	28	19	2	49
Denmark	11	7	2	20
Norway and Sweden	3	...	...	3
Russia	13	1	...	14
Prussia	17	3	...	20
Poland	5	...	...	5
Germany	614	245	89	948
East Indies	1	...	...	1
West Indies	102	46	16	164
Azores	3	...	...	3
Sandwich Islands	1	...	...	1
Canary Islands	3	...	...	3
Africa	...	1	...	1
Asia	...	2	1	3
South America	9	1	1	11
Central America	2	...	...	2
Mexico	1	...	...	1
China	1	...	...	1
Europe	2	...	...	2
United States	1576	287	63	1926
Not stated	165	77	50	292
Total	6447	2680	1184	10311
Born in the United States	1576	287	63	1926
Aliens	4871	2393	1121	8385

Statements exhibiting the *Number and Sex*, *Age*, *Occupation*, and *Country of Birth*, of Passengers arriving in the United States by sea from foreign countries during the year ending September 30, 1821.

I.—ARRIVALS.—Number and Sex.

PORTS AT WHICH THEY ARRIVED.		Males.	Females.	Sex not stated.	Total.
Belfast	Me.	42	6	13	61
Frenchman's Bay	"	19	8	11	38
Portland and Falmouth	"	276	49	33	358
Waldoboro'	"	13	10	22	45
Kennebunk	"	4	...	...	4
Portsmouth	N. H.	18	6	13	37
Boston and Charlestown	Mass.	670	161	182	1013
Newburyport	"	12	3	4	19
Edgartown	"	25	1	...	26
Nantucket	"	22	3	4	29
Plymouth	"	5	...	...	5
Barnstable	"	5	3	2	10
Marblehead	"	2	...	...	2
Bristol	R. I.	38	...	2	40
Providence	"	29	...	...	29
Newport	"	8	1	...	9
New Haven	Ct.	30	11	21	62
Fairfield	"	76	29	34	139
New London	"	4	5	5	14
Oswegatchie	N. Y.	77	59	147	283
New York City	"	2301	649	1088	4038
Perth Amboy	N. J.	43	19	27	89
Philadelphia	Pa.	891	307	585	1783
Baltimore	Md.	862	279	268	1409
Alexandria	D. C.	70	29	52	151
Georgetown	"	10	4	...	14
Norfolk and Portsmouth	Va.	122	40	59	221
Hampton	"	20	9	17	46
Petersburg	"	3	...	...	3
Newbern	N. C.	16	...	...	16
Plymouth	"	5	...	...	5
Charleston	S. C.	506	169	192	867
Savannah	Ga.	154	19	15	188
New Orleans	La.	488	59	44	591
Total		6866	1938	2840	11644

II.—AGE.

AGES.	Males.	Females.	Sex not stated.	Total.
Under 5 years of age . . .	8	6	. . .	14
Between 5 years of age and 10 .	13	9	. . .	22
Between 10 years of age and 15 .	93	41	. . .	134
Between 15 years of age and 20 .	536	227	. . .	763
Between 20 years of age and 25 .	1865	474	. . .	2339
Between 25 years of age and 30 .	1564	406	. . .	1970
Between 30 years of age and 35 .	832	196	. . .	1028
Between 35 years of age and 40 .	713	234	. . .	947
40 years of age and upward . .	1061	335	. . .	1396
Age not stated	181	10	2840	3031
Total . . .	6866	1938	2840	11644

III.—OCCUPATION.

OCCUPATIONS.	Males.	Females.	Sex not stated.	Total.
Merchants	1441	...	...	1441
Farmers	1249	...	...	1249
Mechanics	420	...	...	420
Mariners	477	...	...	477
Miners	2	...	...	2
Laborers	453	...	...	453
Shoemakers	101	...	...	101
Tailors	80	...	...	80
Seamstresses and Milliners	...	15	...	15
Weavers and Spinners	107	...	...	107
Actors and Actresses	19	1	...	20
Physicians	62	...	...	62
Lawyers	20	...	...	20
Clergymen	38	...	...	38
Clerks	114	...	...	114
Painters	21	...	...	21
Printers	12	...	...	12
Millers	15	...	...	15
Engineers	7	...	...	7
Artists	9	...	...	9
Butchers	34	...	...	34
Bakers	61	...	...	61
Hatters	13	...	...	13
Masons	38	...	...	38
Manufacturers	16	...	...	16
Musicians	20	...	...	20
Teachers	33	2	...	35
Servants	78	16	...	94
Other occupations	431	...	...	431
Not stated	1495	1904	2840	6239
Total	6866	1938	2840	11644

IV.—COUNTRY WHERE BORN.

COUNTRIES.	Males.	Females.	Sex not stated.	Total.
England	749	287	...	1036
Ireland	1051	467	...	1518
Scotland	220	73	...	293
Wales	7	4	...	11
Great Britain and Ireland	1276	594	...	1870
British America	153	31	...	184
France	328	42	...	370
Spain	184	7	...	191
Portugal	18	...	...	18
Holland	50	6	...	56
Denmark	10	2	...	12
Prussia	17	1	...	18
Belgium	2	...	...	2
Germany	285	80	...	365
South America	8	...	...	8
Poland	1	...	...	1
Switzerland	85	8	...	93
Russia	7	...	...	7
Mexico	4	...	...	4
Italy	58	4	...	62
West Indies	91	16	...	107
Norway and Sweden	12	...	...	12
Madeira	1	...	...	1
Cape of Good Hope	2	...	...	2
United States	2215	302	...	2517
Not stated	32	14	2840	2886
Total	6866	1938	2840	11644
Born in the United States	2215	302	...	2517
Aliens	4651	1636	2840	9127

Statements exhibiting the *Number and Sex*, *Age*, *Occupation*, and *Country of Birth*, of Passengers arriving in the United States by sea from foreign countries during the year ending September 30, 1822.

I.—ARRIVALS.—Number and Sex.

PORTS AT WHICH THEY ARRIVED.		Males.	Females.	Sex not stated.	Total.
Portland and Falmouth	Me.	55	5	2	62
Waldoboro'	"	20	7	10	37
Belfast	"	16	3	...	19
Portsmouth	N. H.	4	...	...	4
Boston and Charlestown	Mass.	701	138	163	1002
Edgartown	"	35	4	5	44
Marblehead	"	4	1	7	12
Newburyport	"	8	3	10	21
Barnstable	"	117	47	14	178
Plymouth	"	21	1	5	27
Bristol	R. I.	20	3	7	30
Newport	"	15	6	4	25
Providence	"	10	1	2	13
New Haven	Ct.	5	1	...	6
Oswegatchie	N. Y.	23	15	49	87
New York City	"	2443	542	1131	4116
Philadelphia	Pa.	479	99	224	802
Baltimore	Md.	396	123	211	730
Alexandria	D. C.	28	13	17	58
Richmond	Va.	17	8	17	42
Norfolk and Portsmouth	"	100	10	15	125
Newbern	N. C.	6	1	...	7
Charleston	S. C.	350	68	143	561
Savannah	Ga.	58	10	8	76
St. Augustine	Fa.	23	4	...	27
New Orleans	La.	364	36	38	438
Total		5318	1149	2082	8549

II.—AGE

AGES.	Males.	Fe-males.	Sex not stated.	Total.
Under 5 years of age . . .	1	...	...	1
Between 5 years of age and 10 .	10	5	...	15
Between 10 years of age and 15 .	26	9	...	35
Between 15 years of age and 20 .	508	130	...	638
Between 20 years of age and 25 .	1501	263	...	1764
Between 25 years of age and 30 .	1283	284	...	1567
Between 30 years of age and 35 .	683	147	...	830
Between 35 years of age and 40 .	521	110	...	631
40 years of age and upward . .	756	200	...	956
Age not stated	29	1	2082	2112
Total . . .	5318	1149	2082	8549

III.—OCCUPATION.

OCCUPATIONS.	Males.	Females.	Sex not stated.	Total.
Merchants	1431	...	...	1431
Farmers	834	...	...	834
Mechanics	283	...	...	283
Mariners	536	...	...	536
Miners	1	...	...	1
Laborers	414	...	...	414
Shoemakers	71	...	...	71
Tailors	90	...	...	90
Seamstresses and Milliners	...	29	...	29
Weavers and Spinners	146	...	...	146
Actors	6	...	...	6
Physicians	56	...	...	56
Lawyers	23	...	...	23
Clergymen	31	...	...	31
Clerks	74	...	...	74
Painters	9	...	...	9
Printers	15	...	...	15
Millers	14	...	...	14
Engineers	16	...	...	16
Artists	5	...	...	5
Butchers	20	...	...	20
Bakers	30	...	...	30
Hatters	10	...	...	10
Masons	35	...	...	35
Manufacturers	18	...	...	18
Musicians	9	...	...	9
Teachers	21	...	...	21
Servants	11	9	...	20
Other occupations	436	1	...	437
Not stated	673	1110	2082	3865
Total	5318	1149	2082	8549

IV.—COUNTRY WHERE BORN.

COUNTRIES.	Males.	Females.	Sex not stated.	Total.
England	650	206	...	856
Ireland	983	363	...	1346
Scotland	156	42	...	198
Wales	8	5	...	13
Great Britain and Ireland	838	237	...	1075
British America	171	33	...	204
West Indies	132	27	...	159
France	323	28	...	351
Portugal	28	...	...	28
Spain	143	9	...	152
Holland	43	8	...	51
Germany	117	22	...	139
Belgium	10	...	...	10
Denmark	18	...	...	18
Russia	8	2	...	10
Prussia	8	1	...	9
Poland	3	...	...	3
Switzerland	84	26	...	110
Norway and Sweden	10	...	...	10
Italy	31	1	...	32
Sicily	2	...	...	2
Sardinia	1	...	...	1
Turkey	2	2	...	4
Mexico	5	...	...	5
South America	7	...	...	7
Central America	3	...	...	3
Madeira	5	...	...	5
Cape Verde Islands	1	...	...	1
Australia	2	...	...	2
East Indies	1	...	...	1
United States	1502	136	...	1638
Not stated	23	1	2082	2106
Total	5318	1149	2082	8549
Born in the United States	1502	136	...	1638
Aliens	3816	1013	2082	6911

Statements exhibiting the *Number and Sex*, *Age*, *Occupation*, and *Country of Birth*, of Passengers arriving in the United States by sea from foreign countries during the year ending September 30, 1823.

I.—ARRIVALS.—Number and Sex.

PORTS AT WHICH THEY ARRIVED.		Males.	Females.	Sex not stated.	Total.
Belfast	Me.	9	2	5	16
Passamaquoddy	"	18	9	29	56
Frenchman's Bay	"	15	3	3	21
Portland and Falmouth	"	13	...	...	13
Kennebunk	"	2	...	...	2
Boston and Charlestown	Mass.	495	83	94	672
Plymouth	"	2	...	...	2
Nantucket	"	5	...	...	5
New Bedford	"	7	1	1	9
Newburyport	"	32	8	7	47
Marblehead	"	10	...	...	10
Edgartown	"	25	1	4	30
Barnstable	"	99	34	42	175
Salem and Beverly	"	20	5	8	33
Dighton	"	1	...	...	1
New Haven	Ct.	29	15	25	69
New London	"	24	5	30	59
Newport	R. I.	15	3	5	23
Providence	"	27	...	...	27
Bristol and Warren	"	23	2	...	25
Oswegatchie	N. Y.	25	13	17	55
New York City	"	2496	570	1181	4247
Philadelphia	Pa.	289	58	116	463
Baltimore	Md.	363	71	128	562
Alexandria	D. C.	34	8	14	56
Petersburg	Va.	1	...	...	1
Norfolk and Portsmouth	"	54	7	9	70
Richmond	"	10	...	...	10
Plymouth	N. C.	4	...	...	4
Newbern	"	2	...	...	2
Charleston	S. C.	311	43	48	402
Savannah	Ga.	18	4	4	26
St. Augustine	Fa.	10	2	2	14
New Orleans	La.	825	97	136	1058
Total		5313	1044	1908	8265

II.—AGE.

AGES.	Males.	Females.	Sex not stated.	Total.
Between 10 years of age and 15 .	16	1	...	17
Between 15 years of age and 20 .	383	84	...	467
Between 20 years of age and 25 .	1508	269	...	1777
Between 25 years of age and 30 .	1265	275	...	1540
Between 30 years of age and 35 .	723	137	...	860
Between 35 years of age and 40 .	541	129	...	670
40 years of age and upward . .	835	149	...	984
Age not stated	42	...	1908	1950
Total . . .	5313	1044	1908	8265

III.—OCCUPATION.

OCCUPATIONS.	Males.	Females.	Sex not stated.	Total.
Merchants	1427	...	...	1427
Farmers	800	...	...	800
Mechanics	389	...	...	389
Mariners	455	...	...	455
Miners	3	...	...	3
Laborers	338	...	...	338
Shoemakers	46	...	...	46
Tailors	59	...	...	59
Seamstresses and Milliners	...	15	...	15
Weavers and Spinners	85	...	...	85
Actors and Actresses	6	4	...	10
Physicians	73	...	...	73
Lawyers	27	...	...	27
Clergymen	24	...	...	24
Clerks	85	...	...	85
Painters	14	...	...	14
Printers	14	...	...	14
Millers	11	...	...	11
Engineers	5	...	...	5
Artists	13	...	...	13
Butchers	16	...	...	16
Bakers	29	...	...	29
Hatters	5	...	...	5
Masons	26	...	...	26
Manufacturers	11	...	...	11
Musicians	3	...	...	3
Teachers	29	...	...	29
Servants	5	1	...	6
Other occupations	351	7	...	358
Not stated	964	1017	1908	3889
Total	5313	1044	1908	8265

IV.—COUNTRY WHERE BORN.

COUNTRIES.	Males.	Females.	Sex not stated.	Total.
England	663	188	...	851
Ireland	800	251	...	1051
Scotland	140	40	...	180
Wales	53	16	...	69
Great Britain and Ireland	663	194	...	857
British America	143	24	...	167
France	407	53	...	460
Spain	204	16	...	220
Portugal	23	1	...	24
Holland	17	2	...	19
Germany	156	23	...	179
Denmark	4	2	...	6
Belgium	2	...	...	2
Prussia	3	1	...	4
Russia	7	...	...	7
Norway and Sweden	1	...	...	1
Poland	3	...	...	3
Sardinia	1	...	...	1
Switzerland	37	10	...	47
Mexico	35	...	...	35
Italy	30	2	...	32
Turkey	2	...	...	2
Corsica	1	...	...	1
Cape Verde Islands	1	...	...	1
Canary Islands	1	...	...	1
West Indies	140	20	...	160
South America	18	2	...	20
United States	1715	196	...	1911
Not stated	43	3	1908	1954
Total	5313	1044	1908	8265
Born in the United States	1715	196	...	1911
Aliens	3598	848	1908	6354

Statements exhibiting the *Number and Sex*, *Age*, *Occupation*, and *Country of Birth*, of Passengers arriving in the United States by sea from foreign countries during the year ending September 30, 1824.

I.—ARRIVALS.—Number and Sex.

PORTS AT WHICH THEY ARRIVED.		Males.	Females.	Sex not stated.	Total.
Passamaquoddy	Me.	223	66	84	373
Portland and Falmouth . .	"	30	13	12	55
Belfast	"	3	1	...	4
Portsmouth	N. H.	5	...	...	5
Boston and Charlestown .	Mass.	541	113	83	737
Edgartown	"	9	...	...	9
Newburyport	"	18	6	8	32
Barnstable	"	7	9	7	23
Newport	R. I.	9	3	15	27
Providence	"	12	...	...	12
Bristol and Warren . .	"	20	2	...	22
New Haven	Ct.	19	9	4	32
New London	"	21	...	1	22
New York City	N. Y.	3078	861	950	4889
Philadelphia	Pa.	698	231	344	1273
Baltimore	Md.	366	91	153	610
Alexandria	D. C.	65	37	42	144
Norfolk and Portsmouth . .	Va.	75	27	30	132
Richmond	"	8	2	5	15
Newbern	N. C.	7	...	...	7
Charleston	S. C.	143	11	4	158
Savannah	Ga.	17	3	...	20
St. Augustine	Fa.	12	...	...	12
New Orleans	La.	867	76	71	1014
Total . . .		6253	1561	1813	9627

II.—AGE.

AGES.	Males.	Females.	Sex not stated.	Total.
Under 5 years of age . . .	2	2	...	4
Between 5 years of age and 10 .	2	...	...	2
Between 10 years of age and 15 .	66	22	...	88
Between 15 years of age and 20 .	687	237	...	924
Between 20 years of age and 25 .	1702	377	...	2079
Between 25 years of age and 30 .	1498	345	...	1843
Between 30 years of age and 35 .	758	151	...	909
Between 35 years of age and 40 .	642	153	...	795
40 years of age and upward . .	842	264	...	1106
Age not stated	54	10	1813	1877
Total . . .	6253	1561	1813	9627

III.—OCCUPATION.

OCCUPATIONS.	Males.	Females.	Sex not stated.	Total.
Merchants	1926	...	...	1926
Farmers	918	...	...	918
Mechanics	289	...	...	289
Mariners	436	...	...	436
Miners	5	...	...	5
Laborers	381	...	...	381
Shoemakers	57	...	...	57
Tailors	54	...	...	54
Seamstresses and Milliners	...	28	...	28
Weavers and Spinners	121	...	...	121
Actors and Actresses	14	1	...	15
Physicians	70	...	...	70
Lawyers	25	...	...	25
Clergymen	34	...	...	34
Clerks	88	...	...	88
Painters	16	...	...	16
Printers	15	...	...	15
Millers	11	...	...	11
Engineers	20	...	...	20
Artists	3	...	...	3
Butchers	25	...	...	25
Bakers	26	...	...	26
Hatters	7	...	...	7
Masons	29	...	...	29
Manufacturers	10	...	...	10
Musicians	9	...	...	9
Teachers	31	...	...	31
Servants	8	5	...	13
Other occupations	383	2	...	385
Not stated	1242	1525	1813	4580
Total	6253	1561	1813	9627

IV.—COUNTRY WHERE BORN.

COUNTRIES.	Males.	Females.	Sex not stated.	Total.
England	556	157	...	713
Ireland	1133	442	...	1575
Scotland	194	63	...	257
Wales	20	13	...	33
Great Britain and Ireland	754	277	...	1031
British America	114	41	...	155
France	334	43	...	377
Spain	343	16	...	359
Portugal	12	1	...	13
Holland	31	9	...	40
Denmark	11	...	...	11
Prussia	6	...	...	6
Norway and Sweden	9	...	...	9
Poland	4	...	...	4
Russia	7	...	...	7
Belgium	1	...	...	1
Germany	193	31	...	224
Switzerland	179	74	...	253
Italy	41	...	...	41
Sicily	2	...	...	2
Sardinia	2	...	...	2
Greece	5	...	...	5
East Indies	1	...	...	1
Turkey in Asia	2	...	...	2
Canary Islands	1	...	...	1
Mexico	107	3	...	110
West Indies	216	43	...	259
South America	25	...	...	25
Central America	10	...	...	10
United States	1547	168	...	1715
Not stated	393	180	1813	2386
Total	6253	1561	1813	9627
Born in the United States	1547	168	...	1715
Aliens	4706	1393	1813	7912

Statements exhibiting the *Number and Sex*, *Age*, *Occupation*, and *Country of Birth*, of Passengers arriving in the United States by sea from foreign countries during the year ending September 30, 1825.

I.—ARRIVALS.—Number and Sex.

PORTS AT WHICH THEY ARRIVED.		Males.	Females.	Sex not stated.	Total.
Portland and Falmouth . .	Me.	26	12	...	38
Kennebunk	"	6	1	...	7
Passamaquoddy	"	51	17	...	68
Frenchman's Bay	"	4	1	...	5
Portsmouth	N. H.	16	14	...	30
Boston and Charlestown .	Mass.	637	203	18	858
New Bedford	"	12	1	...	13
Newburyport	"	4	...	...	4
Plymouth	"	2	...	...	2
Nantucket	"	12	1	...	13
Barnstable	"	22	17	...	39
Edgartown	"	27	...	...	27
Marblehead	"	4	...	...	4
Providence	R. I.	125	17	18	160
Newport	"	16	4	...	20
Bristol and Warren . .	"	16	...	...	16
New Haven	Ct.	64	29	...	93
New London	"	13	...	...	13
New York City	N. Y.	5430	2029	203	7662
Philadelphia	Pa.	952	364	47	1363
Baltimore	Md.	901	459	5	1365
Alexandria	D. C.	21	15	13	49
Norfolk and Portsmouth . .	Va.	78	14	...	92
Newbern	N. C.	18	...	...	18
Charleston	S. C.	350	88	9	447
Savannah	Ga.	23	...	...	23
New Orleans	La.	376	43	10	429
Total . . .		9206	3329	323	12858

II.—AGE.

AGES.	Males.	Females.	Sex not stated.	Total.
Under 5 years of age . . .	326	316	...	642
Between 5 years of age and 10 .	368	319	...	687
Between 10 years of age and 15 .	310	186	...	496
Between 15 years of age and 20 .	1103	585	...	1688
Between 20 years of age and 25 .	2362	657	...	3019
Between 25 years of age and 30 .	2035	488	...	2523
Between 30 years of age and 35 .	929	227	...	1156
Between 35 years of age and 40 .	794	212	...	1006
40 years of age and upward . .	860	291	...	1151
Age not stated	119	48	323	490
Total . . .	9206	3329	323	12858

III.—OCCUPATION.

OCCUPATIONS.	Males.	Females.	Sex not stated.	Total.
Merchants	1841	...	...	1841
Farmers	1647	...	...	1647
Mechanics	376	...	...	376
Mariners	527	...	...	527
Miners	2	...	...	2
Laborers	650	...	...	650
Shoemakers	49	...	...	49
Tailors	44	...	...	44
Seamstresses and Milliners	...	36	...	36
Weavers and Spinners	162	...	...	162
Actors and Actresses	11	3	...	14
Physicians	87	...	...	87
Lawyers	29	...	...	29
Clergymen	37	...	...	37
Clerks	51	...	...	51
Painters	9	...	...	9
Printers	7	...	...	7
Millers	11	...	...	11
Engineers	24	...	...	24
Artists	9	...	...	9
Butchers	28	...	...	28
Bakers	36	...	...	36
Hatters	11	...	...	11
Masons	38	...	...	38
Manufacturers	5	...	...	5
Musicians	9	...	...	9
Teachers	19	...	...	19
Servants	58	11	...	69
Other occupations	464	1	...	465
Not stated	2965	3278	323	6566
Total	9206	3329	323	12858

IV.—COUNTRY WHERE BORN.

COUNTRIES.	Males.	Females.	Sex not stated.	Total.
England	709	293	...	1002
Ireland	2729	1428	...	4157
Scotland	73	40	...	113
Wales	8	3	...	11
Great Britain and Ireland	1185	515	...	1700
British America	193	121	...	314
France	430	85	...	515
Spain	257	16	...	273
Portugal	12	1	...	13
Denmark	14	...	...	14
Prussia	2	...	...	2
Holland	31	6	...	37
Switzerland	116	50	...	166
Italy	49	9	...	58
Sardinia	14	3	...	17
Belgium	1	...	...	1
Germany	342	106	...	448
Norway and Sweden	3	1	...	4
Poland	...	1	...	1
Russia	10	...	...	10
China	1	...	...	1
Malta	...	1	...	1
Canary Islands	6	...	...	6
Barbary States	1	...	...	1
Azores	1	...	...	1
Madeira	1	...	...	1
Cape Verde Islands	1	...	...	1
Mexico	60	8	...	68
Central America	8	...	...	8
South America	66	1	...	67
West Indies	283	106	...	389
United States	2289	370	...	2659
Not stated	311	165	323	799
Total	9206	3329	323	12858
Born in the United States	2289	370	...	2659
Aliens	6917	2959	323	10199

Statements exhibiting the *Number and Sex*, *Age*, *Occupation*, and *Country of Birth*, of Passengers arriving in the United States by sea from foreign countries during the year ending September 30, 1826.

I.—ARRIVALS.—Number and Sex.

PORTS AT WHICH THEY ARRIVED.		Males.	Females.	Sex not stated.	Total.
Portland and Falmouth . .	Me.	92	15	5	112
Passamaquoddy	"	4	1	...	5
Frenchman's Bay	"	24	42	...	66
Portsmouth	N. H.	10	9	...	19
Boston and Charlestown .	Mass.	919	251	...	1170
Newburyport	"	13	2	...	15
Edgartown	"	37	4	...	41
Barnstable	"	17	11	...	28
Marblehead	"	15	8	...	23
New Bedford	"	74	22	...	96
Dighton	"	3	...	...	3
Plymouth	"	3	7	...	10
Bristol and Warren . .	R. I.	14	...	...	14
Providence	"	22	1	...	23
Newport	"	13	1	...	14
New Haven	Ct.	37	21	...	58
New London	"	5	...	...	5
New York City	N. Y.	5068	1840	...	6908
Philadelphia	Pa.	1593	682	...	2275
Baltimore	Md.	918	493	23	1434
Alexandria	D. C.	13	...	...	13
Norfolk and Portsmouth . .	Va.	85	31	...	116
Newbern	N. C.	15	3	...	18
Charleston	S. C.	253	61	11	325
Savannah	Ga.	15	2	...	17
New Orleans	La.	956	126	18	1100
Total . . .		10218	3633	57	13908

II.—AGE.

AGES.	Males.	Females.	Sex not stated.	Total.
Under 5 years of age . . .	424	422	. . .	846
Between 5 years of age and 10 .	383	380	. . .	763
Between 10 years of age and 15 .	310	342	. . .	652
Between 15 years of age and 20 .	1062	527	. . .	1589
Between 20 years of age and 25 .	2716	651	. . .	3367
Between 25 years of age and 30 .	2269	571	. . .	2840
Between 30 years of age and 35 .	1046	198	. . .	1244
Between 35 years of age and 40 .	786	199	. . .	985
40 years of age and upward . .	1038	243	. . .	1281
Age not stated	184	100	57	341
Total . . .	10218	3633	57	13908

III.—OCCUPATION.

OCCUPATIONS.	Males.	Females.	Sex not stated.	Total.
Merchants	1943	...	...	1943
Farmers	1382	...	...	1382
Mechanics	593	...	...	593
Mariners	555	...	...	555
Miners	17	...	...	17
Laborers	716	...	...	716
Shoemakers	132	...	...	132
Tailors	77	...	...	77
Seamstresses and Milliners	...	69	...	69
Weavers and Spinners	366	...	...	366
Actors and Actresses	1	1	...	2
Physicians	92	...	...	92
Lawyers	25	...	...	25
Clergymen	25	...	...	25
Clerks	75	...	...	75
Painters	14	...	...	14
Printers	27	...	...	27
Millers	17	...	...	17
Engineers	14	...	...	14
Artists	15	...	...	15
Butchers	33	...	...	33
Bakers	57	...	...	57
Hatters	19	...	...	19
Masons	48	...	...	48
Manufacturers	16	...	...	16
Musicians	17	...	...	17
Teachers	14	...	...	14
Servants	35	35	...	70
Other occupations	486	...	...	486
Not stated	3407	3528	57	6992
Total	10218	3633	57	13908

IV.—COUNTRY WHERE BORN.

COUNTRIES.	Males.	Females.	Sex not stated.	Total.
England	1059	400	...	1459
Ireland	2184	1149	...	3333
Scotland	165	65	...	230
Wales	6	...	...	6
Great Britain and Ireland	1871	828	...	2699
British America	166	57	...	223
France	465	80	...	545
Spain	397	39	...	436
Portugal	14	2	...	16
Holland	100	76	...	176
Prussia	15	1	...	16
Denmark	9	1	...	10
Belgium	2	...	...	2
Switzerland	158	87	...	245
Germany	385	110	...	495
Norway and Sweden	14	2	...	16
Russia	3	1	...	4
Italy	45	5	...	50
Sicily	1	...	...	1
Sardinia	6	...	...	6
Greece	4	...	...	4
Canary Islands	10	2	...	12
Cape Verde Islands	1	...	...	1
Turkey in Asia	2	...	...	2
East Indies	1	...	...	1
West Indies	341	86	...	427
Mexico	97	9	...	106
Central America	10	2	...	12
South America	51	12	...	63
United States	2516	555	...	3071
Not stated	120	64	57	241
Total	10218	3633	57	13908
Born in the United States	2516	555	...	3071
Aliens	7702	3078	57	10837

Statements exhibiting the *Number and Sex*, *Age*, *Occupation*, and *Country of Birth*, of Passengers arriving in the United States by sea from foreign countries during the year ending September 30, 1827.

I.—ARRIVALS.—Number and Sex.

PORTS AT WHICH THEY ARRIVED.		Males.	Females.	Sex not stated.	Total.
Passamaquoddy	Me.	75	7	...	82
Portland and Falmouth . .	"	21	6	...	27
Belfast	"	7	...	...	7
Boston and Charlestown .	Mass.	1204	479	175	1858
Barnstable	"	13	8	...	21
Edgartown	"	25	...	...	25
New Bedford	"	12	...	...	12
Newport	R. I.	10	1	...	11
Providence	"	4	...	...	4
New London	Ct.	9	3	...	12
New Haven	"	13	6	...	19
New York City	N. Y.	7940	3813	849	12602
Philadelphia	Pa.	2180	1345	31	3556
Baltimore	Md.	1091	586	29	1706
Alexandria	D. C.	15	...	...	15
Norfolk and Portsmouth . .	Va.	96	12	19	127
Newbern	N. C.	4	...	...	4
Charleston	S. C.	288	48	5	341
St. Augustine	Fa.	5	2	...	7
New Orleans	La.	1153	163	25	1341
Total . . .		14165	6479	1133	21777

4

II.—AGE.

AGES.	Males.	Females.	Sex not stated.	Total.
Under 5 years of age . . .	892	838	. . .	1730
Between 5 years of age and 10 .	630	566	. . .	1196
Between 10 years of age and 15 .	569	410	. . .	979
Between 15 years of age and 20 .	1416	927	. . .	2343
Between 20 years of age and 25 .	3332	1160	. . .	4492
Between 25 years of age and 30 .	3067	995	. . .	4062
Between 30 years of age and 35 .	1351	483	. . .	1834
Between 35 years of age and 40 .	1023	335	. . .	1358
40 years of age and upward . .	1502	646	. . .	2148
Age not stated	383	119	1133	1635
Total . . .	14165	6479	1133	21777

III.—OCCUPATION.

OCCUPATIONS.	Males.	Females.	Sex not stated.	Total.
Merchants	2076	...	...	2076
Farmers	2071	...	...	2071
Mechanics	1056	...	...	1056
Mariners	486	...	...	486
Miners	31	...	...	31
Laborers	1761	...	...	1761
Shoemakers	170	...	...	170
Tailors	139	...	...	139
Seamstresses and Milliners	...	38	...	38
Weavers and Spinners	648	...	...	648
Actors and Actresses	46	10	...	56
Physicians	65	...	...	65
Lawyers	26	...	...	26
Clergymen	42	...	...	42
Clerks	86	...	...	86
Painters	47	...	...	47
Printers	21	...	...	21
Millers	38	...	...	38
Engineers	30	...	...	30
Artists	18	...	...	18
Butchers	18	...	...	18
Bakers	60	...	...	60
Hatters	23	...	...	23
Masons	130	...	...	130
Manufacturers	35	...	...	35
Musicians	26	...	...	26
Teachers	29	...	...	29
Servants	74	62	...	136
Other occupations	715	2	...	717
Not stated	4198	6367	1133	11698
Total	14165	6479	1133	21777

IV.—COUNTRY WHERE BORN.

COUNTRIES.	Males.	Females.	Sex not stated.	Total.
England	1742	779	...	2521
Ireland	2137	1145	...	3282
Scotland	312	148	...	460
Great Britain and Ireland	4874	2815	...	7689
British America	124	41	...	165
France	878	402	...	1280
Spain	375	39	...	414
Portugal	6	1	...	7
Holland	149	96	...	245
Belgium	7	...	...	7
Prussia	6	1	...	7
Denmark	14	1	...	15
Switzerland	173	124	...	297
Germany	339	86	...	425
Poland	1	...	...	1
Russia	18	1	...	19
Italy	33	2	...	35
Corsica	1	...	...	1
Norway and Sweden	11	2	...	13
Turkey in Asia	1	...	...	1
East Indies	1	...	...	1
Azores	4	...	...	4
Madeira	1	...	...	1
Barbary States	2	1	...	3
Africa	...	1	...	1
South Sea Islands	44	35	...	79
West Indies	197	30	...	227
South America	47	7	...	54
Mexico	115	12	...	127
Central America	7	...	...	7
United States	2362	540	...	2902
Not stated	184	170	1133	1487
Total	14165	6479	1133	21777
Born in the United States	2362	540	...	2902
Aliens	11803	5939	1133	18875

Statements exhibiting the *Number and Sex*, *Age*, *Occupation*, and *Country of Birth*, of Passengers arriving in the United States by sea from foreign countries during the year ending September 30, 1828.

I.—ARRIVALS.—Number and Sex.

PORTS AT WHICH THEY ARRIVED.		Males.	Females.	Sex not stated.	Total.
Passamaquoddy	. Me.	536	316	. . .	852
Boston and Charlestown .	Mass.	923	573	. . .	1496
New York City	N. Y.	12473	7386	1	19860
Philadelphia	. Pa.	2185	1263	52	3500
Alexandria	D. C.	72	45	. . .	117
Baltimore	. Md.	1296	647	8	1951
Norfolk and Portsmouth .	. Va.	65	31	. . .	96
Newbern	N. C.	3	2	. . .	5
Charleston	S. C.	272	77	. . .	349
New Orleans	La.	1621	337	. . .	1958
Total . . .		19446	10677	61	30184

II.—AGE.

AGES.	Males.	Females.	Sex not stated.	Total.
Under 5 years of age . . .	1748	1573	...	3321
Between 5 years of age and 10 .	1488	1388	...	2876
Between 10 years of age and 15 .	1038	882	...	1920
Between 15 years of age and 20 .	2129	1580	...	3709
Between 20 years of age and 25 .	3939	1653	...	5592
Between 25 years of age and 30 .	3285	1283	...	4568
Between 30 years of age and 35 .	1749	648	...	2397
Between 35 years of age and 40 .	1475	656	...	2131
40 years of age and upward . .	2098	938	...	3036
Age not stated	497	76	61	634
Total . . .	19446	10677	61	30184

III.—OCCUPATION.

OCCUPATIONS.	Males.	Females.	Sex not stated.	Total.
Merchants	2328	...	...	2328
Farmers	2542	...	...	2542
Mechanics	1334	...	...	1334
Mariners	468	...	...	468
Miners	50	...	...	50
Laborers	2628	...	...	2628
Shoemakers	267	...	...	267
Tailors	206	...	...	206
Seamstresses and Milliners	...	107	...	107
Weavers and Spinners	759	7	...	766
Actors and Actresses	19	12	...	31
Physicians	112	...	...	112
Lawyers	31	...	...	31
Clergymen	70	...	...	70
Clerks	106	...	...	106
Painters	44	...	...	44
Printers	34	...	...	34
Millers	35	...	...	35
Engineers	33	...	...	33
Artists	26	...	...	26
Butchers	61	...	...	61
Bakers	140	...	...	140
Hatters	26	...	...	26
Masons	162	...	...	162
Manufacturers	29	...	...	29
Musicians	26	2	...	28
Teachers	33	...	...	33
Servants	173	248	...	421
Other occupations	781	9	...	790
Not stated	6923	10292	61	17276
Total	19446	10677	61	30184

IV.—COUNTRY WHERE BORN.

COUNTRIES.	Males.	Females.	Sex not stated.	Total.
England	1823	912	...	2735
Ireland	3166	2100	...	5266
Scotland	646	395	...	1041
Wales	8	9	...	17
Great Britain and Ireland	5330	3451	...	8781
British America	164	103	...	267
France	1746	1097	...	2843
Spain	181	28	...	209
Portugal	14	...	...	14
Prussia	40	5	...	45
Holland	152	111	...	263
Denmark	25	25	...	50
Belgium	2	...	...	2
Germany	1115	691	...	1806
Switzerland	950	642	...	1592
Norway and Sweden	7	3	...	10
Poland	1	...	...	1
Russia	6	1	...	7
Italy	28	2	...	30
Greece	5	2	...	7
Turkey	6	...	...	6
Sicily	4	...	...	4
East Indies	3	...	...	3
Canary Islands	5	...	...	5
Azores	3	...	...	3
Madeira	7	2	...	9
Africa	6	...	...	6
South America	63	14	...	77
Central America	5	...	...	5
Mexico	973	116	...	1089
West Indies	539	113	...	652
United States	2185	617	...	2802
Not stated	238	238	61	537
Total	19446	10677	61	30184
Born in the United States	2185	617	...	2802
Aliens	17261	10060	61	27382

Statements exhibiting the *Number and Sex*, *Age*, *Occupation*, and *Country of Birth*, of Passengers arriving in the United States by sea from foreign countries during the year ending September 30, 1829.

I.—ARRIVALS.—Number and Sex.

PORTS AT WHICH THEY ARRIVED.		Males.	Females.	Sex not stated.	Total.
Portland and Falmouth	Me.	45	8	...	53
Passamaquoddy	"	588	261	...	849
Belfast	"	7	3	...	10
Boston and Charlestown	Mass.	1015	576	4	1595
Dighton	"	7	...	...	7
Nantucket	"	2	...	...	2
Newburyport	"	3	1	...	4
Providence	R. I.	26	3	...	29
New London	Ct.	3	...	...	3
New Haven	"	18	13	...	31
New York City	N. Y.	5903	2810	6101	14814
Perth Amboy	N. J.	79	26	...	105
Philadelphia	Pa.	898	570	...	1468
Baltimore	Md.	1085	606	...	1691
Alexandria	D. C.	271	50	...	321
Norfolk and Portsmouth	Va.	197	45	...	242
Newbern	N. C.	5	...	...	5
Washington	"	9	...	...	9
Charleston	S. C.	199	32	...	231
New Orleans	La.	2578	466	...	3044
Total		12938	5470	6105	24513

II.—AGE.

AGES.	Males.	Fe-males.	Sex not stated.	Total.
Under 5 years of age . . .	802	712	. . .	1514
Between 5 years of age and 10 .	649	526	. . .	1175
Between 10 years of age and 15 .	568	429	. . .	997
Between 15 years of age and 20 .	1055	703	. . .	1758
Between 20 years of age and 25 .	2347	831	. . .	3178
Between 25 years of age and 30 .	2605	798	. . .	3403
Between 30 years of age and 35 .	1470	448	. . .	1918
Between 35 years of age and 40 .	1034	312	. . .	1346
40 years of age and upward . .	1342	422	. . .	1764
Age not stated	1066	289	6105	7460
Total . . .	12938	5470	6105	24513

III.—OCCUPATION.

OCCUPATIONS.	Males.	Females.	Sex not stated.	Total.
Merchants	2661	...	...	2661
Farmers	1260	4	...	1264
Mechanics	854	...	...	854
Mariners	408	...	...	408
Miners	141	...	...	141
Laborers	1885	...	...	1885
Shoemakers	111	...	...	111
Tailors	127	...	...	127
Seamstresses and Milliners	...	40	...	40
Weavers and Spinners	268	80	...	348
Actors and Actresses	19	1	...	20
Physicians	96	...	...	96
Lawyers	15	...	...	15
Clergymen	54	...	...	54
Clerks	108	...	...	108
Painters	31	...	...	31
Printers	21	...	...	21
Millers	38	...	...	38
Engineers	28	...	...	28
Artists	14	...	...	14
Butchers	44	...	...	44
Bakers	76	...	...	76
Hatters	12	...	...	12
Masons	178	...	...	178
Manufacturers	14	...	...	14
Musicians	14	...	...	14
Teachers	38	1	...	39
Servants	219	118	...	337
Other occupations	705	12	...	717
Not stated	3499	5214	6105	14818
Total	12938	5470	6105	24513

IV.—COUNTRY WHERE BORN.

COUNTRIES.	Males.	Fe-males.	Sex not stated.	Total.
England	1545	604	...	2149
Ireland	1963	1143	...	3106
Scotland	89	22	...	111
Wales	3	...	...	3
Great Britain and Ireland	3254	1971	...	5225
British America	258	151	...	409
France	420	162	...	582
Spain	173	29	...	202
Portugal	6	3	...	9
Italy	15	1	...	16
Greece	1	...	...	1
Sicily	6	1	...	7
Denmark	11	6	...	17
Holland	113	56	...	169
Prussia	12	3	...	15
Germany	392	190	...	582
Switzerland	179	135	...	314
Russia	1	...	...	1
Norway and Sweden	10	3	...	13
East Indies	1	...	...	1
Turkey in Asia	1	...	...	1
China	1	...	...	1
Canary Islands	171	72	...	243
Azores	1	...	...	1
Madeira	44	2	...	46
Liberia	1	...	...	1
West Indies	430	87	...	517
Mexico	1933	357	...	2290
South America	60	13	...	73
Central America	8	2	...	10
United States	1635	358	...	1993
Not stated	201	99	6105	6405
Total	12938	5470	6105	24513
Born in the United States	1635	358	...	1993
Aliens	11303	5112	6105	22520

Statements exhibiting the *Number and Sex*, *Age*, *Occupation*, and *Country of Birth*, of Passengers arriving in the United States by sea from foreign countries during the year ending September 30, 1830.

I.—ARRIVALS.—Number and Sex.

PORTS AT WHICH THEY ARRIVED.		Males.	Females.	Sex not stated.	Total.
Portland and Falmouth	Me.	69	53	...	122
Portsmouth	N. H.	13	7	...	20
Boston and Charlestown	Mass.	1053	467	...	1520
Edgartown	"	48	56	...	104
New London	Ct.	57	54	...	111
New Haven	"	27	18	...	45
New York City	N. Y.	...	...	13748	13748
Perth Amboy	N. J.	31	43	...	74
Philadelphia	Pa.	1208	682	...	1890
Wilmington	Del.	30	35	...	65
Baltimore	Md.	2374	1569	...	3943
Alexandria	D. C.	209	24	...	233
Norfolk and Portsmouth	Va.	389	134	...	523
Charleston	S. C.	121	31	...	152
New Orleans	La.	1885	402	...	2287
Total		7514	3575	13748	24837

II.—AGE.

AGES.	Males.	Females.	Sex not stated.	Total.
Under 5 years of age . . .	621	619	...	1240
Between 5 years of age and 10 .	479	494	...	973
Between 10 years of age and 15 .	363	302	...	665
Between 15 years of age and 20 .	573	367	...	940
Between 20 years of age and 25 .	1291	448	...	1739
Between 25 years of age and 30 .	1310	386	...	1696
Between 30 years of age and 35 .	853	253	...	1106
Between 35 years of age and 40 .	656	210	...	866
40 years of age and upward . .	866	307	...	1173
Age not stated	502	189	13748	14439
Total . . .	7514	3575	13748	24837

III.—OCCUPATION.

OCCUPATIONS.	Males.	Females.	Sex not stated.	Total.
Merchants	1427	...	...	1427
Farmers	1424	...	...	1424
Mechanics	942	...	...	942
Mariners	311	...	...	311
Miners	85	...	...	85
Laborers	720	...	...	720
Shoemakers	43	...	...	43
Tailors	44	...	...	44
Seamstresses and Milliners	...	1	...	1
Weavers and Spinners	98	...	...	98
Actors	7	...	...	7
Physicians	49	...	...	49
Lawyers	17	...	...	17
Clergymen	36	...	...	36
Clerks	32	...	...	32
Painters	10	...	...	10
Printers	8	...	...	8
Millers	2	...	...	2
Engineers	37	...	...	37
Artists	18	...	...	18
Butchers	14	...	...	14
Bakers	22	...	...	22
Hatters	6	...	...	6
Masons	82	...	...	82
Manufacturers	8	...	...	8
Musicians	3	...	...	3
Teachers	6	...	...	6
Servants	22	...	...	22
Other occupations	340	3	...	343
Not stated	1701	3571	13748	19020
Total	7514	3575	13748	24837

IV.—COUNTRY WHERE BORN.

COUNTRIES.	Males.	Females.	Sex not stated.	Total.
England	448	285	...	733
Ireland	462	285	...	747
Scotland	25	4	...	29
Wales	7	...	...	7
Great Britain and Ireland	1591	767	...	2358
British America	112	77	...	189
France	712	462	...	1174
Spain	18	3	...	21
Portugal	3	...	...	3
Switzerland	62	47	...	109
Italy	8	...	...	8
Turkey	2	...	...	2
Greece	3	...	...	3
Sicily	1	...	...	1
Holland	16	6	...	22
Prussia	1	3	...	4
Germany	1157	815	...	1972
Denmark	11	5	...	16
Norway and Sweden	2	1	...	3
Poland	2	...	...	2
Russia	3	...	...	3
Madeira	4	3	...	7
Azores	1	...	...	1
Africa	2	...	...	2
Central America	43	7	...	50
West Indies	771	166	...	937
Mexico	868	115	...	983
South America	79	58	...	137
United States	1075	440	...	1515
Not stated	25	26	13748	13799
Total	7514	3575	13748	24837
Born in the United States	1075	440	...	1515
Aliens	6439	3135	13748	23322

Statements exhibiting the *Number and Sex*, *Age*, *Occupation*, and *Country of Birth*, of Passengers arriving in the United States by sea from foreign countries during the year ending September 30, 1831.

I.—ARRIVALS.—Number and Sex.

PORTS AT WHICH THEY ARRIVED.		Males.	Females.	Total.
Portland and Falmouth	Me.	16	2	18
Passamaquoddy	"	48	23	71
Boston and Charlestown . . .	Mass.	1049	368	1417
Plymouth	"	17	9	26
Newburyport	"	5	. . .	5
New Bedford	"	16	7	23
Edgartown	"	9	1	10
New Haven	Ct.	27	6	33
New York City	N. Y.	6943	3794	10737
Perth Amboy	N. J.	28	29	57
Philadelphia	Pa.	2272	1536	3808
Baltimore	Md.	2338	1373	3711
Alexandria	D. C.	83	18	101
Richmond	Va.	5	4	9
Norfolk and Portsmouth	"	440	112	552
East River	"	4	. . .	4
Charleston	S. C.	69	38	107
New Orleans	La.	2548	643	3191
Total . . .		15917	7963	23880

II.—AGE.

AGES.	Males.	Females.	Total.
Under 5 years of age	1366	1353	2719
Between 5 years of age and 10 . . .	1200	1134	2334
Between 10 years of age and 15 . . .	1140	847	1987
Between 15 years of age and 20 . . .	1415	832	2247
Between 20 years of age and 25 . . .	2791	1046	3837
Between 25 years of age and 30 . . .	2546	835	3381
Between 30 years of age and 35 . . .	1781	653	2434
Between 35 years of age and 40 . . .	1228	471	1699
40 years of age and upward	1334	529	1863
Age not stated	1116	263	1379
Total	15917	7963	23880

III.—OCCUPATION.

OCCUPATIONS.	Males.	Females.	Total.
Merchants	2368	...	2368
Farmers	2685	...	2685
Mechanics	1241	...	1241
Mariners	461	...	461
Miners	18	...	18
Laborers	928	...	928
Shoemakers	125	...	125
Tailors	82	...	82
Seamstresses and Milliners	...	7	7
Weavers and Spinners	166	...	166
Actors and Actresses	10	13	23
Physicians	73	...	73
Lawyers	15	...	15
Clergymen	35	...	35
Clerks	65	...	65
Painters	10	...	10
Printers	34	...	34
Millers	17	...	17
Engineers	8	...	8
Artists	18	...	18
Butchers	11	...	11
Bakers	46	...	46
Hatters	12	...	12
Masons	60	...	60
Manufacturers	20	...	20
Musicians	10	...	10
Teachers	9	...	9
Servants	84	31	115
Other occupations	316	17	333
Not stated	6990	7895	14885
Total	15917	7963	23880

IV.—COUNTRY WHERE BORN.

COUNTRIES.	Males.	Females.	Total.
England	169	82	251
Ireland	1035	612	1647
Scotland	157	69	226
Wales	81	50	131
Great Britain and Ireland	3678	2314	5992
British America	132	44	176
France	1332	706	2038
Spain	32	5	37
Italy	25	3	28
Switzerland	63	...	63
Belgium	1	...	1
Holland	147	28	175
Prussia	13	5	18
Germany	1511	884	2395
Denmark	20	3	23
Norway and Sweden	8	5	13
Russia	...	1	1
Cape Verde Islands	1	...	1
Madeira	1	...	1
Africa	2	...	2
Sandwich Islands	1	...	1
East Indies	1	...	1
West Indies	1066	215	1281
Mexico	624	68	692
Central America	3	...	3
South America	35	7	42
United States	1008	239	1247
Not stated	4771	2623	7394
Total	15917	7963	23880
Born in the United States	1008	239	1247
Aliens	14909	7724	22633

Statements exhibiting the *Number and Sex*, *Age*, *Occupation*, and *Country of Birth*, of Passengers arriving in the United States by sea from foreign countries during the year ending September 30, 1832.

I.—ARRIVALS.—Number and Sex.

PORTS AT WHICH THEY ARRIVED.		Males.	Females.	Total.
Portland and Falmouth	Me.	26	8	34
Passamaquoddy	"	1682	689	2371
Bath	"	26	28	54
Portsmouth	N. H.	3	...	3
Boston and Charlestown	Mass.	1627	746	2373
New Bedford	"	53	23	76
Edgartown	"	18	2	20
Newburyport	"	2	...	2
Nantucket	"	2	...	2
Marblehead	"	4	...	4
Plymouth	"	3	...	3
Providence	R. I.	18	9	27
Newport	"	16	8	24
New Haven	Ct.	64	34	98
New London	"	35	27	62
Sag Harbor	N. Y.	65	6	71
New York City	"	19103	9811	28914
Perth Amboy	N. J.	299	246	545
Philadelphia	Pa.	2899	1848	4747
Baltimore	Md.	6065	3914	9979
Alexandria	D. C.	93	25	118
Richmond	Va.	2	3	5
Norfolk and Portsmouth	"	139	52	191
Mobile	Ala.	142	89	231
New Orleans	La.	3213	1184	4397
Total		35599	18752	54351

II.—AGE.

AGES.	Males.	Females.	Total.
Under 5 years of age	3258	2666	5924
Between 5 years of age and 10 . . .	2947	2362	5309
Between 10 years of age and 15 . . .	3233	2019	5252
Between 15 years of age and 20 . . .	4088	2270	6358
Between 20 years of age and 25 . . .	5814	2509	8323
Between 25 years of age and 30 . . .	5384	2162	7546
Between 30 years of age and 35 . . .	3588	1569	5157
Between 35 years of age and 40 . . .	2471	1214	3685
40 years of age and upward	2974	1299	4273
Age not stated	1842	682	2524
Total	35599	18752	54351

III.—OCCUPATION.

OCCUPATIONS.	Males.	Females.	Total.
Merchants	4747	...	4747
Farmers	7845	...	7845
Mechanics	4145	...	4145
Mariners	791	...	791
Miners	61	...	61
Laborers	3323	...	3323
Shoemakers	536	...	536
Tailors	578	...	578
Seamstresses and Milliners	...	9	9
Weavers and Spinners	1807	4	1811
Actors and Actresses	12	1	13
Physicians	39	...	39
Lawyers	28	...	28
Clergymen	30	...	30
Clerks	56	...	56
Painters	23	...	23
Printers	178	...	178
Millers	84	...	84
Engineers	35	...	35
Artists	6	...	6
Butchers	143	...	143
Bakers	273	...	273
Hatters	52	...	52
Masons	399	...	399
Manufacturers	16	...	16
Musicians	28	...	28
Teachers	16	...	16
Servants	46	10	56
Other occupations	579	...	579
Not stated	9723	18728	28451
Total	35599	18752	54351

IV.—COUNTRY WHERE BORN.

COUNTRIES.	Males.	Females.	Total.
England	598	346	944
Ireland	3217	1903	5120
Scotland	113	45	158
Great Britain and Ireland	7129	4416	11545
British America	430	178	608
France	3702	1659	5361
Spain	74	32	106
Portugal	5	...	5
Italy	2	...	2
Switzerland	77	52	129
Greece	1	...	1
Sicily	1	...	1
Corsica	1	1	2
Holland	130	75	205
Prussia	13	13	26
Germany	6120	4048	10168
Denmark	19	2	21
Norway and Sweden	184	129	313
Russia	32	20	52
Poland	24	10	34
East Indies	3	1	4
Azores	4	1	5
Africa	1	1	2
Mexico	757	70	827
Central America	5	1	6
West Indies	943	313	1256
South America	120	54	174
United States	1003	169	1172
Not stated	10891	5213	16104
Total	35599	18752	54351
Born in the United States	1003	169	1172
Aliens	34596	18583	53179

Statements exhibiting the *Number and Sex*, *Age*, *Occupation*, and *Country of Birth*, of Passengers arriving in the United States by sea from foreign countries during the quarter ending December 31, 1832.

I.—ARRIVALS.—Number and Sex.

PORTS AT WHICH THEY ARRIVED.		Males.	Females.	Sex not stated.	Total.
Boston and Charlestown .	Mass.	541	330	100	971
New York City	N. Y.	4150	2182	. . .	6332
Total . . .		4691	2512	100	7303

II.—AGE.

AGES.	Males.	Females.	Sex not stated.	Total.
Under 5 years of age . . .	326	289	...	615
Between 5 years of age and 10 .	346	277	...	623
Between 10 years of age and 15 .	436	272	...	708
Between 15 years of age and 20 .	599	276	...	875
Between 20 years of age and 25 .	594	278	...	872
Between 25 years of age and 30 .	550	239	...	789
Between 30 years of age and 35 .	480	207	...	687
Between 35 years of age and 40 .	393	158	...	551
40 years of age and upward . .	295	130	...	425
Age not stated	672	386	100	1158
Total . . .	4691	2512	100	7303

III.—OCCUPATION.

OCCUPATIONS.	Males.	Females.	Sex not stated.	Total.
Merchants	677	...	...	677
Farmers	657	...	...	657
Mechanics	510	...	...	510
Mariners	73	...	...	73
Tailors	141	...	...	141
Shoemakers	98	...	...	98
Weavers and Spinners	226	...	...	226
Physicians	5	...	...	5
Artists	11	...	...	11
Masons	38	...	...	38
Painters	16	...	...	16
Butchers	16	...	...	16
Bakers	25	...	...	25
Other occupations	22	...	...	22
Not stated	2176	2512	100	4788
Total	4691	2512	100	7303

IV.—COUNTRY WHERE BORN.

COUNTRIES.	Males.	Fe-males.	Sex not stated.	Total.
Not stated	4691	2512	100	7303

Statements exhibiting the *Number and Sex*, *Age*, *Occupation*, and *Country of Birth*, of Passengers arriving in the United States by sea from foreign countries during the year ending December 31, 1833.

I.—ARRIVALS.—Number and Sex.

PORTS AT WHICH THEY ARRIVED.		Males.	Females.	Total.
Passamaquoddy	Me.	1607	574	2181
Waldoboro'	"	8	8	16
Portland and Falmouth	"	30	5	35
Portsmouth	N. H.	1	2	3
Boston and Charlestown	Mass.	2089	1151	3240
Newburyport	"	5	...	5
Plymouth	"	4	1	5
Edgartown	"	72	55	127
Marblehead	"	6	12	18
New Bedford	"	21	25	46
Nantucket	"	3	...	3
Dighton	"	26	10	36
Providence	R. I.	20	7	27
New London	Ct.	42	39	81
New Haven	"	46	29	75
New York City	N. Y.	29176	10264	39440
Philadelphia	Pa.	2550	1666	4216
Wilmington	Del.	232	207	439
Baltimore	Md.	2952	1667	4619
Alexandria	D. C.	79	48	127
Norfolk and Portsmouth	Va.	131	56	187
Charleston	S. C.	147	67	214
New Orleans	La.	3301	1484	4785
Total		42548	17377	59925

II.—AGE.

AGES.	Males.	Females.	Total.
Under 5 years of age	3652	2102	5754
Between 5 years of age and 10	3704	1957	5661
Between 10 years of age and 15	4231	1779	6010
Between 15 years of age and 20	4682	2253	6935
Between 20 years of age and 25	6308	2594	8902
Between 25 years of age and 30	5888	2093	7981
Between 30 years of age and 35	4550	1579	6129
Between 35 years of age and 40	3784	1271	5055
40 years of age and upward	3592	1263	4855
Age not stated	2157	486	2643
Total	42548	17377	59925

III.—OCCUPATION.

OCCUPATIONS.	Males.	Females.	Total.
Merchants	4913	...	4913
Farmers	6618	...	6618
Mechanics	4130	...	4130
Mariners	1872	...	1872
Miners	75	...	75
Laborers	4109	...	4109
Shoemakers	829	...	829
Tailors	1066	...	1066
Seamstresses and Milliners	...	19	19
Weavers and Spinners	3429	...	3429
Actors	6	...	6
Physicians	297	...	297
Lawyers	27	...	27
Clergymen	27	...	27
Clerks	18	...	18
Painters	209	...	209
Printers	203	...	203
Millers	2	...	2
Engineers	41	...	41
Artists	78	...	78
Butchers	178	...	178
Bakers	100	...	100
Hatters	1	...	1
Masons	624	...	624
Manufacturers	4	...	4
Musicians	9	...	9
Teachers	15	...	15
Servants	80	2	82
Other occupations	722	...	722
Not stated	12866	17356	30222
Total	45548	17377	59925

IV.—COUNTRY WHERE BORN.

COUNTRIES.	Males.	Females.	Total.
England	2522	444	2966
Ireland	3089	1422	4511
Scotland	1898	23	1921
Wales	16	13	29
Great Britain and Ireland	2410	1727	4137
British America	786	408	1194
France	3392	1290	4682
Spain	487	29	516
Portugal	632	1	633
Switzerland	630	4	634
Italy	1693	...	1693
Sicily	4	2	6
Malta	3	2	5
Greece	1	...	1
Turkey	1	...	1
Holland	33	6	39
Denmark	160	13	173
Germany	5134	1689	6823
Prussia	165	...	165
Poland	1	...	1
Norway and Sweden	9	7	16
Russia	156	3	159
East Indies	2	1	3
Canary Islands	3	...	3
Azores	2	1	3
Madeira	2	...	2
Africa	1	...	1
South America	18	9	27
Central America	17	1	18
West Indies	1152	112	1264
Mexico	705	74	779
United States	1002	283	1285
Not stated	16422	9813	26235
Total	42548	17377	59925
Born in the United States	1002	283	1285
Aliens	41546	17094	58640

Statements exhibiting the *Number and Sex*, *Age*, *Occupation*, and *Country of Birth*, of Passengers arriving in the United States by sea from foreign countries during the year ending December 31, 1834.

I.—ARRIVALS.—Number and Sex.

PORTS AT WHICH THEY ARRIVED.	Males.	Females.	Sex not stated.	Total.
Portland and Falmouth . Me.	65	24	...	89
Passamaquoddy . . . . "	667	21	2352	3040
Portsmouth . . . . N. H.	4	4	...	8
Boston and Charlestown, Mass.	1764	1060	107	2931
Gloucester . . . . "	4	....	...	4
Fall River . . . . "	28	29	...	57
Marblehead . . . . "	3	3	...	6
New Bedford . . . "	15	1	...	16
Newburyport . . . "	3	....	...	3
Newport . . . . . . R. I.	10	3	...	13
Providence . . . . "	46	18	...	64
New London . . . . . Ct.	5	2	...	7
New Haven . . . . . . "	39	26	...	65
New York City . . . N. Y.	27903	16571	1579	46053
Sag Harbor . . . . "	79	44	...	123
Philadelphia . . . . . Pa.	2417	1753	...	4170
Baltimore . . . . . Md.	4465	2448	...	6913
Alexandria . . . . D. C.	45	17	...	62
Norfolk and Portsmouth . Va.	138	62	...	200
Charleston . . . . S. C.	72	17	...	89
New Orleans . . . . La.	2958	1077	...	4035
Total . . .	40730	23180	4038	67948

II.—AGE.

AGES.	Males.	Females.	Sex not stated.	Total.
Under 5 years of age . . .	3050	2827	164	6041
Between 5 years of age and 10	2454	2364	148	4966
Between 10 years of age and 15	2398	1868	110	4376
Between 15 years of age and 20	3656	2903	205	6764
Between 20 years of age and 25	8450	4181	812	13443
Between 25 years of age and 30	7067	2739	769	10575
Between 30 years of age and 35	3968	1700	327	5995
Between 35 years of age and 40	4036	1879	119	6034
40 years of age and upward .	4236	2336	246	6818
Age not stated	1415	383	1138	2936
Total . . .	40730	23180	4038	67948

III.—OCCUPATION.

OCCUPATIONS.	Males.	Females.	Sex not stated.	Total.
Merchants	3021	....	...	3021
Farmers	7160	....	...	7160
Mechanics	3642	....	...	3642
Mariners	484	....	...	484
Miners	132	....	...	132
Laborers	2874	....	...	2874
Shoemakers	373	....	...	373
Tailors	317	....	...	317
Seamstresses and Milliners	....	228	...	228
Weavers and Spinners	177	4	757	938
Actors	6	....	...	6
Physicians	173	....	...	173
Lawyers	60	....	...	60
Clergymen	94	....	...	94
Clerks	182	....	...	182
Painters	105	....	...	105
Printers	50	....	...	50
Millers	78	....	...	78
Engineers	60	....	...	60
Artists	101	4	...	105
Butchers	82	....	...	82
Bakers	117	....	...	117
Hatters	48	....	...	48
Masons	314	....	...	314
Manufacturers	40	....	...	40
Musicians	62	....	...	62
Teachers	60	1	...	61
Servants	49	31	1156	1236
Other occupations	1178	4	...	1182
Not stated	19691	22908	2125	44724
Total	40730	23180	4038	67948

IV.—COUNTRY WHERE BORN.

COUNTRIES.	Males.	Females.	Sex not stated.	Total.
England	648	430	51	1129
Ireland	4121	2636	15	6772
Scotland	57	53	...	110
Wales	1	....	...	1
Great Britain and Ireland	16362	10590	...	26952
British America	599	409	12	1020
France	1892	1097	...	2989
Spain	99	8	...	107
Portugal	40	4	...	44
Switzerland	849	540	...	1389
Belgium	3	....	...	3
Prussia	24	8	...	32
Denmark	20	4	...	24
Holland	45	42	...	87
Germany	11439	6215	...	17654
Norway and Sweden	38	4	...	42
Russia	12	3	...	15
Poland	51	3	...	54
Italy	83	20	...	103
Sicily	1	....	...	1
Sardinia	1	....	...	1
Turkey	1	....	...	1
Cape Verde Islands	2	1	...	3
Azores	1	....	...	1
Canaries	3	....	...	3
Madeira	24	1	...	25
Africa	1	....	...	1
East Indies	5	1	...	6
West Indies	610	181	...	791
Mexico	795	90	...	885
Central America	8	1	...	9
South America	60	13	1	74
United States	1934	640	9	2583
Not stated	901	186	3950	5037
Total	40730	23180	4038	67948
Born in the United States	1934	640	9	2583
Aliens	38796	22540	4029	65365

Statements exhibiting the *Number and Sex*, *Age*, *Occupation*, and *Country of Birth*, of Passengers arriving in the United States by sea from foreign countries during the year ending December 31, 1835.

I.—ARRIVALS.—Number and Sex.

PORTS AT WHICH THEY ARRIVED.	Males.	Females.	Sex not stated.	Total.
Passamaquoddy . . . . Me.	2259	1023	...	3282
Portland and Falmouth . "	24	9	...	33
Boston and Charlestown, Mass.	1851	1152	165	3168
New Bedford . . . "	21	6	...	27
Edgartown . . . . "	23	9	...	32
Newburyport . . . "	14	12	...	26
Gloucester . . . . "	1	....	...	1
Nantucket . . . . "	1	....	...	1
Dighton . . . . . "	83	58	...	141
Newport . . . . . R. I.	9	6	...	15
Providence . . . . "	4	2	...	6
New London. . . . . Ct.	15	6	...	21
New Haven . . . . . "	57	22	...	79
New York City . . . N. Y.	20025	12690	...	32715
Newark . . . . . . N. J.	1	....	...	1
Philadelphia . . . . . Pa.	1034	671	...	1705
Baltimore . . . . . . Md.	2299	1267	...	3566
Alexandria . . . . D. C.	24	5	...	29
Norfolk and Portsmouth . Va.	33	....	...	33
Washington . . . . N. C.	3	....	...	3
Charleston . . . . S. C.	211	61	8	280
New Orleans . . . . . La.	2760	792	...	3552
Total . . .	30752	17791	173	48716

II.—AGE.

AGES.	Males.	Females.	Sex not stated.	Total.
Under 5 years of age . . .	2128	2017	. . .	4145
Between 5 years of age and 10	1731	1578	. . .	3309
Between 10 years of age and 15	1751	1430	. . .	3181
Between 15 years of age and 20	3063	2709	. . .	5772
Between 20 years of age and 25	6478	3216	. . .	9694
Between 25 years of age and 30	5595	2190	. . .	7785
Between 30 years of age and 35	3157	1341	. . .	4498
Between 35 years of age and 40	3230	1433	. . .	4663
40 years of age and upward .	3568	1863	. . .	5431
Age not stated	51	14	173	238
Total . . .	30752	17791	173	48716

III.—OCCUPATION.

OCCUPATIONS.	Males.	Females.	Sex not stated.	Total.
Merchants	3875	....	...	3875
Farmers	6117	....	...	6117
Mechanics	4776	....	...	4776
Mariners	727	....	...	727
Miners	2	....	...	2
Laborers	2897	....	...	2897
Shoemakers	1	....	...	1
Tailors	7	....	...	7
Seamstresses and Milliners	....	216	...	216
Weavers and Spinners	7	....	...	7
Actors and Actresses	12	1	...	13
Physicians	202	....	...	202
Lawyers	74	....	...	74
Clergymen	110	....	...	110
Clerks	171	....	...	171
Painters	4	....	...	4
Printers	3	....	...	3
Millers	3	....	...	3
Engineers	61	....	...	61
Artists	33	....	...	33
Butchers	1	....	...	1
Bakers	3	....	...	3
Hatters	1	....	...	1
Manufacturers	22	....	...	22
Musicians	16	....	...	16
Teachers	39	....	...	39
Servants	196	403	...	599
Other occupations	270	....	...	270
Not stated	11122	17171	173	28466
Total	30752	17791	173	48716

IV.—COUNTRY WHERE BORN.

COUNTRIES.	Males.	Females.	Sex not stated.	Total.
England	340	128	...	468
Ireland	2658	2490	...	5148
Scotland	32	31	...	63
Wales	10	6	...	16
Great Britain and Ireland	14322	9743	137	24202
British America	783	410	...	1193
France	2030	666	...	2696
Spain	154	29	...	183
Portugal	24	5	...	29
Switzerland	326	222	...	548
Belgium	1	....	...	1
Holland	82	42	...	124
Prussia	53	13	...	66
Germany	5352	2893	...	8245
Denmark	24	13	...	37
Poland	52	2	...	54
Norway and Sweden	23	8	...	31
Russia	7	2	...	9
Italy	45	11	...	56
Greece	7	....	...	7
Sicily	2	2	...	4
China	3	3	2	8
East Indies	8	....	...	8
Asia	1	....	...	1
Cape Verde Islands	10	1	...	11
St. Helena	1	....	...	1
Azores	2	....	...	2
Madeira	4	....	...	4
Africa	10	4	...	14
Sandwich Islands	2	1	...	3
South America	125	18	2	145
Central America	4	....	...	4
Mexico	912	120	...	1032
West Indies	776	159	3	938
United States	2556	764	22	3342
Not stated	11	5	7	23
Total	30752	17791	173	48716
Born in the United States	2556	764	22	3342
Aliens	28196	17027	151	45374

Statements exhibiting the *Number and Sex*, *Age*, *Occupation*, and *Country of Birth*, of Passengers arriving in the United States by sea from foreign countries during the year ending December 31, 1836.

I.—ARRIVALS.—Number and Sex.

PORTS AT WHICH THEY ARRIVED.	Males.	Females.	Sex not stated.	Total.
Passamaquoddy . . . . Me.	1581	445	...	2026
Portland and Falmouth . "	1327	700	...	2027
Portsmouth . . . . N. H.	2	2	...	4
Boston and Charlestown, Mass.	1989	1114	155	3258
New Bedford . . . "	25	13	...	38
Dighton . . . . . "	28	16	...	44
Edgartown . . . . "	6	....	...	6
Newburyport . . . "	5	....	...	5
Marblehead . . . . "	3	....	...	3
Newport . . . . . R. I.	12	10	...	22
Providence . . . . "	26	21	...	47
New London . . . . . Ct.	9	6	...	15
New Haven . . . . . "	32	17	...	49
New York City . . . N. Y.	36548	21400	669	58617
Perth Amboy . . . N. J.	307	187	...	494
Philadelphia . . . . . Pa.	1558	949	...	2507
Baltimore . . . . . Md.	3698	2431	...	6129
Alexandria . . . . D. C.	19	3	...	22
Norfolk and Portsmouth . Va.	100	63	...	163
Richmond . . . . . "	106	40	...	146
Washington . . . . N. C.	2	....	...	2
Newbern . . . . . "	4	1	...	5
Charleston . . . . S. C.	234	94	...	328
Key West . . . . . Fla.	43	6	...	49
New Orleans . . . . La.	3795	1171	...	4966
Total . . .	51459	28689	824	80972

II.—AGE.

AGES.	Males.	Females.	Sex not stated.	Total.
Under 5 years of age . . .	3241	3070	. . .	6311
Between 5 years of age and 10	2672	2550	. . .	5222
Between 10 years of age and 15	2764	2368	. . .	5132
Between 15 years of age and 20	5029	3850	. . .	8879
Between 20 years of age and 25	13139	6248	. . .	19387
Between 25 years of age and 30	9789	3829	. . .	13618
Between 30 years of age and 35	5442	2272	. . .	7714
Between 35 years of age and 40	3547	1593	. . .	5140
40 years of age and upward .	5273	2868	. . .	8141
Age not stated	563	41	824	1428
Total . . .	51459	28689	824	80972

III.—OCCUPATION.

OCCUPATIONS.	Males.	Females.	Sex not stated.	Total.
Merchants	3379	....	...	3379
Farmers	8770	....	...	8770
Mechanics	7838	....	...	7838
Mariners	722	....	...	722
Laborers	8749	....	...	8749
Tailors	21	....	...	21
Seamstresses and Milliners	....	210	...	210
Actors	2	....	...	2
Physicians	229	....	...	229
Lawyers	27	....	...	27
Clergymen	130	....	...	130
Clerks	73	....	...	73
Millers	1	....	...	1
Engineers	14	....	...	14
Artists	58	....	...	58
Musicians	6	....	...	6
Teachers	20	....	...	20
Servants	3	36	...	39
Other occupations	201	....	...	201
Not stated	21216	28443	824	50483
Total	51459	28689	824	80972

IV.—COUNTRY WHERE BORN.

COUNTRIES.	Males.	Females.	Sex not stated.	Total.
England	276	144	...	420
Ireland	1433	719	...	2152
Scotland	74	32	...	106
Wales	2	....	...	2
Great Britain and Ireland	25197	15807	...	41004
British America	1854	960	...	2814
France	2972	1471	...	4443
Spain	154	26	...	180
Portugal	25	4	...	29
Switzerland	310	135	...	445
Prussia	386	182	...	568
Holland	213	88	...	301
Germany	12657	7482	...	20139
Italy	88	19	...	107
Sicily	7	1	...	8
Malta	2	....	...	2
Greece	27	1	...	28
Turkey	3	....	...	3
Russia	2	....	...	2
Poland	47	6	...	53
Norway and Sweden	43	14	...	57
Denmark	303	113	...	416
Africa	6	....	...	6
Madeira	2	3	...	5
East Indies	4	....	...	4
Mexico	725	73	...	798
West Indies	926	252	...	1178
South America	126	20	...	146
Sandwich Islands	1	1	...	2
United States	3594	1136	...	4730
Not stated	....	....	824	824
Total	51459	28689	824	80972
Born in the United States	3594	1136	...	4730
Aliens	47865	27553	824	76242

Statements exhibiting the *Number and Sex*, *Age*, *Occupation*, and *Country of Birth*, of Passengers arriving in the United States by sea from foreign countries during the year ending December 31, 1837.

I.—ARRIVALS.—Number and Sex.

PORTS AT WHICH THEY ARRIVED.		Males.	Females.	Sex not stated.	Total.
Passamaquoddy	Me.	2418	1146	. . .	3564
Portland and Falmouth .	"	62	27	. . .	89
Portsmouth	N. H.	1	. . . .	. . .	1
Boston and Charlestown,	Mass.	2242	1364	67	3673
New Bedford . . .	"	20	6	. . .	26
Edgartown	"	19	15	. . .	34
Nantucket	"	4	. . . .	. . .	4
Fall River	"	18	10	. . .	28
Providence	R. I.	57	33	. . .	90
Newport	"	15	12	. . .	27
New Haven	Ct.	27	15	. . .	42
New London	"	5	. . . .	. . .	5
New York City . . .	N. Y.	31474	17419	2783	51676
Perth Amboy . . .	N. J.	3031	1975	. . .	5006
Philadelphia	Pa.	2481	1713	. . .	4194
Wilmington	Del.	109	94	. . .	203
Baltimore	Md.	4080	2552	. . .	6632
Alexandria	D. C.	7	6	. . .	13
Norfolk and Portsmouth .	Va.	102	44	. . .	146
Richmond	"	99	48	. . .	147
Newbern	N. C.	2	. . . .	. . .	2
Washington	"	1	5	. . .	6
Charleston	S. C.	310	83	. . .	393
Key West	Fla.	214	61	. . .	275
New Orleans	La.	6605	2078	. . .	8683
Total . . .		53403	28706	2850	84959

II.—AGE.

AGES.	Males.	Females.	Sex not stated.	Total.
Under 5 years of age . . .	3457	2788	...	6245
Between 5 years of age and 10	2600	2256	...	4856
Between 10 years of age and 15	2597	2316	...	4913
Between 15 years of age and 20	4841	4116	...	8957
Between 20 years of age and 25	11977	6197	...	18174
Between 25 years of age and 30	10354	4052	...	14406
Between 30 years of age and 35	5549	2161	...	7710
Between 35 years of age and 40	3593	1472	...	5065
40 years of age and upward .	5448	2973	...	8421
Age not stated	2987	375	2850	6212
Total . . .	53403	28706	2850	84959

III.—OCCUPATION.

OCCUPATIONS.	Males.	Females.	Sex not stated.	Total.
Merchants	3893	....	...	3893
Farmers	10835	....	...	10835
Mechanics	7296	....	...	7296
Mariners	775	....	...	775
Miners	2	....	...	2
Laborers	9095	....	...	9095
Tailors	37	....	...	37
Seamstresses and Milliners	....	223	...	223
Weavers and Spinners	2	....	...	2
Physicians	258	....	...	258
Lawyers	32	....	...	32
Clergymen	121	....	...	121
Clerks	124	....	...	124
Millers	1	....	...	1
Engineers	19	....	...	19
Artists	69	....	...	69
Bakers	4	....	...	4
Musicians	26	....	...	26
Teachers	16	....	...	16
Servants	4	116	...	120
Other occupations	382	7	...	389
Not stated	20412	28360	2850	51622
Total	53403	28706	2850	84959

IV.—COUNTRY WHERE BORN.

COUNTRIES.	Males.	Females.	Sex not stated.	Total.
England	613	283	...	896
Ireland	428	309	...	737
Scotland	10	4	...	14
Wales	....	6	...	6
Great Britain and Ireland	23710	15363	...	39073
British America	816	463	...	1279
France	3461	1613	...	5074
Spain	197	33	...	230
Portugal	26	8	...	34
Switzerland	250	133	...	383
Prussia	482	222	...	704
Germany	15085	7951	...	23036
Holland	226	86	...	312
Denmark	68	41	...	109
Norway and Sweden	179	111	...	290
Poland	72	9	...	81
Russia	17	2	...	19
Italy	32	4	...	36
Greece	5	....	...	5
East Indies	6	5	...	11
Africa	2	....	...	2
Madeira	4	1	...	5
South America	76	15	...	91
Central America	2	2	...	4
Mexico	542	85	...	627
West Indies	1277	350	...	1627
United States	4566	1053	...	5619
Not stated	1251	554	2850	4655
Total	53403	28706	2850	84959
Born in the United States	4566	1053	...	5619
Aliens	48837	27653	2850	79340

Statements exhibiting the *Number and Sex*, *Age*, *Occupation*, and *Country of Birth*, of Passengers arriving in the United States by sea from foreign countries during the year ending December 31, 1838.

I.—ARRIVALS.—Number and Sex.

PORTS AT WHICH THEY ARRIVED.	Males.	Females.	Sex not stated.	Total.
Passamaquoddy . . . . Me.	1577	634	. . .	2211
Portland and Falmouth . "	36	9	. . .	45
Boston and Charlestown, Mass.	1270	782	18	2070
Newburyport . . . "	5	1	. . .	6
Fall River . . . . "	23	27	. . .	50
Nantucket . . . . "	10	. . . .	. . .	10
New Bedford . . . "	18	4	. . .	22
Newport . . . . . . R. I.	30	8	. . .	38
Providence . . . . "	19	17	. . .	36
New Haven . . . . . Ct.	25	8	. . .	33
New London . . . . . "	11	1	. . .	12
New York City . . . N. Y.	14628	8570	1737	24935
Philadelphia . . . . . Pa.	1177	982	. . .	2159
Wilmington . . . . . Del.	98	90	. . .	188
Baltimore . . . . . Md.	3231	2003	. . .	5234
Alexandria . . . . D. C.	8	1	. . .	9
Norfolk and Portsmouth . Va.	23	9	. . .	32
Charleston . . . . S. C.	356	121	. . .	477
Key West . . . . . Fla.	118	40	. . .	158
New Orleans . . . . La.	5841	1593	. . .	7434
Total . . .	28504	14900	1755	45159

II.—AGE.

AGES.	Males.	Females.	Sex not stated.	Total.
Under 5 years of age . . .	1738	1632	. . .	3370
Between 5 years of age and 10	1456	1322	. . .	2778
Between 10 years of age and 15	1482	1192	. . .	2674
Between 15 years of age and 20	2591	2093	. . .	4684
Between 20 years of age and 25	6028	2636	. . .	8664
Between 25 years of age and 30	5708	2065	. . .	7773
Between 30 years of age and 35	3153	1177	. . .	4330
Between 35 years of age and 40	2358	904	. . .	3262
40 years of age and upward .	3883	1865	. . .	5748
Age not stated	107	14	1755	1876
Total . . .	28504	14900	1755	45159

III.—OCCUPATION.

OCCUPATIONS.	Males.	Females.	Sex not stated.	Total.
Merchants	4005	....	...	4005
Farmers	6667	....	...	6667
Mechanics	4643	....	...	4643
Mariners	734	....	...	734
Miners	14	....	...	14
Laborers	3684	....	...	3684
Tailors	1	....	...	1
Seamstresses and Milliners	....	88	...	88
Weavers and Spinners	3	....	...	3
Physicians	237	....	...	237
Lawyers	61	....	...	61
Clergymen	96	....	...	96
Clerks	173	....	...	173
Millers	1	....	...	1
Engineers	13	....	...	13
Artists	39	....	...	39
Manufacturers	5	....	...	5
Musicians	3	....	...	3
Teachers	21	2	...	23
Servants	10	32	...	42
Other occupations	115	1	...	116
Not stated	7979	14777	1755	24511
Total	28504	14900	1755	45159

IV.—COUNTRY WHERE BORN.

COUNTRIES.	Males.	Females.	Sex not stated.	Total.
England	104	53	...	157
Ireland	700	525	...	1225
Scotland	29	19	...	48
Great Britain and Ireland	9992	6643	...	16635
British America	1034	442	...	1476
France	2564	1111	...	3675
Spain	175	27	...	202
Portugal	20	4	...	24
Switzerland	95	28	...	123
Belgium	9	5	...	14
Prussia	197	117	...	314
Germany	7097	4272	...	11369
Holland	20	7	...	27
Denmark	38	14	...	52
Italy	67	15	...	82
Greece	4	....	...	4
Sicily	4	....	...	4
Corsica	1	....	...	1
Russia	13	....	...	13
Poland	36	5	...	41
Norway and Sweden	44	16	...	60
Egypt	4	....	...	4
Morocco	4	....	...	4
Africa	2	....	...	2
Madeira	1	1	...	2
Azores	2	4	...	6
Isle of France	2	....	...	2
East Indies	1	....	...	1
South America	54	18	...	72
Mexico	177	34	...	211
West Indies	967	264	...	1231
United States	5030	1215	...	6245
Not stated	17	61	1755	1833
Total	28504	14900	1755	45159
Born in the United States	5030	1215	...	6245
Aliens	23474	13685	1755	38914

Statements exhibiting the *Number and Sex*, *Age*, *Occupation*, and *Country of Birth*, of Passengers arriving in the United States by sea from foreign countries during the year ending December 31, 1839.

I.—ARRIVALS.—Number and Sex.

PORTS AT WHICH THEY ARRIVED.	Males.	Females.	Sex not stated.	Total.
Passamaquoddy . . . . Me.	1984	735	...	2719
Portland and Falmouth . "	42	14	...	56
Boston and Charlestown, Mass.	1783	1251	12	3046
New Bedford . . . "	13	3	...	16
Newburyport . . . "	5	....	...	5
Nantucket . . . . "	1	....	...	1
Fall River . . . . "	21	8	...	29
New Haven . . . . . Ct.	19	10	...	29
New London . . . . . "	3	....	...	3
Providence . . . . R. I.	19	11	...	30
Newport . . . . . "	37	15	...	52
New York City . . . N. Y.	29985	17703	...	47688
Philadelphia . . . . . Pa.	2266	1683	...	3949
Baltimore . . . . . . Md.	3728	2353	...	6081
Alexandria . . . . D. C.	32	6	...	38
Norfolk and Portsmouth . Va.	11	....	...	11
Charleston . . . . S. C.	406	139	...	545
Key West . . . . . . Fla.	50	12	...	62
New Orleans . . . . . La.	7795	2511	...	10306
Total . . .	48200	26454	12	74666

II.—AGE.

AGES.	Males.	Fe-males.	Sex not stated.	Total.
Under 5 years of age . . .	2678	2164	. . .	4842
Between 5 years of age and 10	2532	2212	. . .	4744
Between 10 years of age and 15	3078	2503	. . .	5581
Between 15 years of age and 20	5297	3873	. . .	9170
Between 20 years of age and 25	9316	4711	. . .	14027
Between 25 years of age and 30	9436	3717	. . .	13153
Between 30 years of age and 35	6225	2710	. . .	8935
Between 35 years of age and 40	3840	1938	. . .	5778
40 years of age and upward .	4811	2390	. . .	7201
Age not stated	987	236	12	1235
Total . . .	48200	26454	12	74666

III.—OCCUPATION.

OCCUPATIONS.	Males.	Females.	Sex not stated.	Total.
Merchants	5692	....	...	5692
Farmers	12410	....	...	12410
Mechanics	8887	....	...	8887
Mariners	570	....	...	570
Miners	23	....	...	23
Laborers	7870	....	...	7870
Shoemakers	1	....	...	1
Seamstresses and Milliners	....	312	...	312
Weavers and Spinners	1	....	...	1
Actors and Actresses	8	5	...	13
Physicians	255	....	...	255
Lawyers	76	....	...	76
Clergymen	145	....	...	145
Clerks	208	....	...	208
Printers	2	....	...	2
Millers	1	....	...	1
Engineers	20	....	...	20
Bakers	1	....	...	1
Musicians	1	....	...	1
Teachers	53	1	...	54
Artists	40	....	...	40
Servants	46	53	...	99
Other occupations	96	1	...	97
Not stated	11794	26082	12	37888
Total	48200	26454	12	74666

IV.—COUNTRY WHERE BORN.

COUNTRIES.	Males.	Females.	Sex not stated.	Total.
England	46	16	...	62
Ireland	796	403	...	1199
Great Britain and Ireland	19999	12974	...	32973
British America	1329	597	...	1926
France	4835	2363	...	7198
Spain	333	95	...	428
Portugal	16	3	...	19
Switzerland	430	177	...	607
Belgium	1	....	...	1
Prussia	769	465	...	1234
Germany	12445	7349	...	19794
Holland	53	32	...	85
Denmark	44	12	...	56
Norway and Sweden	188	136	...	324
Poland	34	12	...	46
Russia	4	3	...	7
Turkey	1	....	...	1
Italy	64	12	...	76
Sicily	2	....	...	2
Sardinia	6	....	...	6
Corsica	2	....	...	2
Malta	20	8	...	28
Australia	1	....	...	1
Liberia	6	2	...	8
Azores	4	3	...	7
South America	38	11	...	49
Mexico	320	33	...	353
West Indies	1035	254	...	1289
United States	5268	1329	...	6597
Not stated	111	165	12	288
Total	48200	26454	12	74666
Born in the United States	5268	1329	...	6597
Aliens	42932	25125	12	68069

Statements exhibiting the *Number and Sex*, *Age*, *Occupation*, and *Country of Birth*, of Passengers arriving in the United States by sea from foreign countries during the year ending December 31, 1840.

I.—ARRIVALS.—Number and Sex.

PORTS AT WHICH THEY ARRIVED.	Males.	Females.	Sex not stated.	Total.
Passamaquoddy . . . . Me.	1834	724	. . .	2558
Portland and Falmouth . "	26	14	. . .	40
Portsmouth . . . . N. H.	22	22	. . .	44
Boston and Charlestown, Mass.	3556	1754	51	5361
New Bedford . . . "	26	4	. . .	30
Newburyport . . . "	8	. . . .	. . .	8
Fall River . . . . "	7	3	. . .	10
Newport . . . . . R. I.	20	4	. . .	24
Providence . . . . "	11	8	. . .	19
New London . . . . . Ct.	1	. . . .	. . .	1
New Haven . . . . . "	36	13	. . .	49
New York City . . . N. Y.	37867	22742	. . .	60609
Philadelphia . . . . . Pa.	2321	1758	. . .	4079
Wilmington . . . . . Del.	273	198	. . .	471
Baltimore . . . . . Md.	4440	2831	. . .	7271
Alexandria . . . . D. C.	23	15	. . .	38
Norfolk and Portsmouth . Va.	152	95	. . .	247
Plymouth . . . . N. C.	1	. . . .	. . .	1
Charleston . . . . S. C.	181	43	. . .	224
Key West . . . . . Fla.	36	2	. . .	38
New Orleans . . . . La.	8157	2928	. . .	11085
Total . . .	58998	33158	51	92207

II.—AGE.

AGES.	Males.	Females.	Sex not stated.	Total.
Under 5 years of age . . .	3769	2779	. . .	6548
Between 5 years of age and 10	3825	2975	. . .	6800
Between 10 years of age and 15	4927	3452	. . .	8379
Between 15 years of age and 20	7297	5036	. . .	12333
Between 20 years of age and 25	10914	5778	. . .	16692
Between 25 years of age and 30	11228	5015	. . .	16243
Between 30 years of age and 35	6477	3093	. . .	9570
Between 35 years of age and 40	5269	2354	. . .	7623
40 years of age and upward .	4964	2592	. . .	7556
Age not stated	328	84	51	463
Total . . .	58998	33158	51	92207

III.—OCCUPATION.

OCCUPATIONS.	Males.	Females.	Sex not stated.	Total.
Merchants	5311	....	...	5311
Mechanics	9474	....	...	9474
Farmers	18476	....	...	18476
Mariners	795	....	...	795
Miners	41	....	...	41
Laborers	9640	....	...	9640
Tailors	2	....	...	2
Seamstresses and Milliners	....	360	...	360
Weavers and Spinners	11	6	...	17
Physicians	191	....	...	191
Lawyers	61	....	...	61
Clergymen	144	....	...	144
Clerks	73	....	...	73
Millers	1	....	...	1
Engineers	40	....	...	40
Artists	53	3	...	56
Butchers	1	....	...	1
Musicians	3	1	...	4
Teachers	11	3	...	14
Printers	2	....	...	2
Actors and Actresses	6	5	...	11
Shoemakers	3	....	...	3
Painters	2	....	...	2
Servants	62	121	...	183
Other occupations	93	....	...	93
Not stated	14502	32659	51	47212
Total	58998	33158	51	92207

IV.—COUNTRY WHERE BORN.

COUNTRIES.	Males.	Females.	Sex not stated.	Total.
England	219	99	...	318
Ireland	386	291	...	677
Scotland	20	1	...	21
Great Britain and Ireland	25045	15982	...	41027
British America	1341	597	...	1938
France	4843	2576	...	7419
Spain	110	26	...	136
Portugal	9	3	...	12
Switzerland	293	207	...	500
Belgium	1	1	...	2
Prussia	684	439	...	1123
Germany	18121	10460	...	28581
Holland	36	21	...	57
Denmark	96	56	...	152
Norway and Sweden	40	15	...	55
Poland	5	....	...	5
Turkey	1	....	...	1
Greece	3	....	...	3
Italy	27	1	...	28
Sicily	9	....	...	9
East Indies	1	....	...	1
Australia	2	....	...	2
Africa	4	2	...	6
Azores	3	2	...	5
Madeira	8	....	...	8
South America	31	5	...	36
Mexico	346	49	...	395
West Indies	1164	282	...	1446
United States	6115	2026	...	8141
Not stated	35	17	51	103
Total	58998	33158	51	92207
Born in the United States	6115	2026	...	8141
Aliens	52883	31132	51	84066

Statements exhibiting the *Number and Sex*, *Age*, *Occupation*, and *Country of Birth*, of Passengers arriving in the United States by sea from foreign countries during the year ending December 31, 1841.

I.—ARRIVALS.—Number and Sex.

PORTS AT WHICH THEY ARRIVED.	Males.	Females.	Sex not stated.	Total.
Passamaquoddy . . . . Me.	2253	1074	...	3327
Portland and Falmouth . "	63	22	...	85
Portsmouth . . . . N. H.	13	11	...	24
Boston and Charlestown, Mass.	5165	3293	176	8634
New Bedford . . . "	12	13	...	25
Nantucket . . . . "	5	....	...	5
Plymouth . . . . "	11	3	...	14
Providence . . . . R. I.	30	11	...	41
Newport . . . . . "	15	2	...	17
New Haven . . . . . Ct.	32	14	...	46
New London . . . . . "	2	5	...	7
New York City . . . N. Y.	33489	22396	...	55885
Wilmington . . . . . Del.	455	547	...	1002
Philadelphia . . . . . Pa.	1721	1295	...	3016
Baltimore . . . . . Md.	2732	1779	...	4511
Alexandria . . . . D. C.	114	84	...	198
Norfolk and Portsmouth . Va.	15	10	...	25
Charleston . . . . S. C.	161	43	...	204
Key West . . . . . Fla.	25	14	...	39
New Orleans . . . . La.	7502	3198	...	10700
Total . . .	53815	33814	176	87805

II.—AGE.

AGES.	Males.	Females.	Sex not stated.	Total.
Under 5 years of age . . .	4049	3328	. . .	7377
Between 5 years of age and 10	3336	2753	. . .	6089
Between 10 years of age and 15	3460	2806	. . .	6266
Between 15 years of age and 20	5344	4633	. . .	9977
Between 20 years of age and 25	9772	5750	. . .	15522
Between 25 years of age and 30	10390	5142	. . .	15532
Between 30 years of age and 35	6619	3429	. . .	10048
Between 35 years of age and 40	5058	2727	. . .	7785
40 years of age and upward .	5582	3008	. . .	8590
Age not stated	205	238	176	619
Total . . .	53815	33814	176	87805

III.—OCCUPATION.

OCCUPATIONS.	Males.	Females.	Sex not stated.	Total.
Merchants	5267	....	...	5267
Mechanics	9842	....	...	9842
Farmers	12343	....	...	12343
Mariners	810	....	...	810
Miners	12	....	...	12
Laborers	11423	....	...	11423
Shoemakers	7	....	...	7
Tailors	11	....	...	11
Seamstresses and Milliners	....	228	...	228
Actors and Actresses	27	13	...	40
Physicians	208	....	...	208
Lawyers	62	....	...	62
Clergymen	179	....	...	179
Clerks	86	....	...	86
Millers	1	....	...	1
Engineers	30	....	...	30
Artists	35	....	...	35
Butchers	29	....	...	29
Bakers	1	....	...	1
Masons	2	....	...	2
Manufacturers	52	....	...	52
Musicians	6	1	...	7
Teachers	10	....	...	10
Servants	97	826	...	923
Other occupations	137	32	...	169
Not stated	13138	32714	176	46028
Total	53815	33814	176	87805

IV.—COUNTRY WHERE BORN.

COUNTRIES.	Males.	Females.	Sex not stated.	Total.
England	119	28	...	147
Ireland	1868	1423	...	3291
Scotland	28	7	...	35
Wales	43	12	...	55
Great Britain and Ireland	29434	20998	...	50432
British America	1201	615	...	1816
France	3431	1575	...	5006
Spain	170	45	...	215
Portugal	7	....	...	7
Switzerland	471	280	...	751
Belgium	69	37	...	106
Prussia	899	665	...	1564
Germany	8431	5296	...	13727
Holland	124	90	...	214
Denmark	19	12	...	31
Norway and Sweden	130	65	...	195
Poland	10	5	...	15
Russia	101	73	...	174
Turkey	6	....	...	6
Italy	140	26	...	166
Sicily	12	1	...	13
Malta	42	24	...	66
East Indies	1	....	...	1
China	2	....	...	2
Africa	8	6	...	14
Azores	3	....	...	3
Sandwich Islands	....	3	...	3
South America	57	162	...	219
Mexico	289	63	...	352
West Indies	848	194	...	1042
United States	5733	1783	...	7516
Not stated	119	326	176	621
Total	53815	33814	176	87805
Born in the United States	5733	1783	...	7516
Aliens	48082	32031	176	80289

Statements exhibiting the *Number and Sex*, *Age*, *Occupation*, and *Country of Birth*, of Passengers arriving in the United States by sea from foreign countries during the year ending December 31, 1842.

I.—ARRIVALS.—Number and Sex.

PORTS AT WHICH THEY ARRIVED.	Males.	Females.	Sex not stated.	Total.
Passamaquoddy . . . . Me.	2801	1585	. . .	4386
Portland and Falmouth . "	367	329	. . .	696
Kennebunk . . . . . "	2	. . . .	. . .	2
Portsmouth . . . . N. H.	129	106	. . .	235
Boston and Charlestown, Mass.	4651	2991	379	8021
Fall River . . . . "	46	55	1	102
New Bedford . . . "	22	. . . .	. . .	22
Marblehead . . . . "	4	. . . .	. . .	4
Providence . . . . R. I.	38	18	. . .	56
Newport . . . . . "	15	3	. . .	18
New Haven . . . . . Ct.	32	22	. . .	54
New York City . . . N. Y.	44499	29515	. . .	74014
Philadelphia . . . . . Pa.	1835	1534	. . .	3369
Wilmington . . . . . Del.	694	778	. . .	1472
Baltimore . . . . . Md.	3169	2141	. . .	5310
Alexandria . . . . D. C.	48	25	. . .	73
Norfolk and Portsmouth . Va.	8	. . . .	. . .	8
Charleston . . . . S. C.	129	40	. . .	169
Key West . . . . . Fla.	39	7	1	47
New Orleans . . . . La.	8596	4326	. . .	12922
Total . . .	67124	43475	381	110980

II.—AGE.

AGES.	Males.	Females.	Sex not stated.	Total.
Under 5 years of age . . .	5609	5530	. . .	11139
Between 5 years of age and 10	4034	3768	. . .	7802
Between 10 years of age and 15	3471	3104	. . .	6575
Between 15 years of age and 20	7789	7437	. . .	15226
Between 20 years of age and 25	15126	8473	. . .	23599
Between 25 years of age and 30	13374	6347	. . .	19721
Between 30 years of age and 35	6142	2714	. . .	8856
Between 35 years of age and 40	4830	2267	. . .	7097
40 years of age and upward .	6213	3496	. . .	9709
Age not stated	536	339	381	1256
Total . . .	67124	43475	381	110980

III.—OCCUPATION.

OCCUPATIONS.	Males.	Females.	Sex not stated.	Total.
Merchants	4976	....	...	4976
Mechanics	13121	....	...	13121
Farmers	12966	....	...	12966
Laborers	15951	....	...	15951
Mariners	766	....	...	766
Miners	38	....	...	38
Shoemakers	1	....	...	1
Tailors	3	....	...	3
Seamstresses and Milliners	....	463	...	463
Weavers and Spinners	1	....	...	1
Actors and Actresses	6	2	...	8
Physicians	257	....	...	257
Clergymen	151	....	...	151
Clerks	101	....	...	101
Lawyers	89	....	...	89
Musicians	40	....	...	40
Butchers	7	....	...	7
Teachers	93	1	...	94
Engineers	48	....	...	48
Artists	98	7	...	105
Millers	2	....	...	2
Printers	2	....	...	2
Servants	46	1218	...	1264
Other occupations	316	....	...	316
Not stated	18045	41784	381	60210
Total	67124	43475	381	110980

IV.—COUNTRY WHERE BORN.

COUNTRIES.	Males.	Females.	Sex not stated.	Total.
England	982	761	...	1743
Ireland	2727	2117	...	4844
Scotland	12	12	...	24
Wales	24	14	...	38
Great Britain and Ireland	39136	27562	...	66698
British America	1265	813	...	2078
France	2982	1522	...	4504
Spain	105	17	...	122
Portugal	14	1	...	15
Prussia	1211	872	...	2083
Belgium	34	10	...	44
Switzerland	318	165	...	483
Germany	11079	7208	...	18287
Holland	188	142	...	330
Denmark	28	7	...	35
Poland	8	2	...	10
Norway and Sweden	311	242	...	553
Russia	22	6	...	28
Turkey	2	....	...	2
Greece	1	....	...	1
Italy	76	17	...	93
Malta	1	....	...	1
Sardinia	1	2	...	3
Corsica	....	1	...	1
Sicily	4	....	...	4
East Indies	2	....	...	2
China	....	4	...	4
Persia	1	....	...	1
Canary Islands	1	....	...	1
Azores	3	1	...	4
Africa	2	1	...	3
South America	79	23	...	102
Central America	1	....	...	1
Mexico	365	38	...	403
West Indies	1155	255	...	1410
United States	4847	1568	...	6415
Not stated	137	92	381	610
Total	67124	43475	381	110980
Born in the United States	4847	1568	...	6415
Aliens	62277	41907	381	104565

Statements exhibiting the *Number and Sex*, *Age*, *Occupation*, and *Country of Birth*, of Passengers arriving in the United States by sea from foreign countries during the first three quarters of 1843.

I.—ARRIVALS.—Number and Sex.

PORTS AT WHICH THEY ARRIVED.	Males.	Females.	Sex not stated.	Total.
Passamaquoddy . . . . Me.	1543	846	...	2389
Portsmouth . . . . N. H.	16	4	...	20
Boston and Charlestown, Mass.	2450	1201	3	3654
New Bedford . . . "	12	1	...	13
Nantucket . . . . "	1	....	...	1
Marblehead . . . . "	1	....	...	1
Providence . . . . R. I.	11	11	...	22
Bristol and Warren . "	1	....	...	1
Newport . . . . . "	4	....	...	4
New Haven . . . . . Ct.	26	8	...	34
New York City . . . N. Y.	22115	16815	...	38930
Philadelphia . . . . . Pa.	1147	1150	...	2297
Baltimore . . . . . Md.	1714	1239	...	2953
Alexandria . . . . D. C.	11	4	...	15
Norfolk and Portsmouth . Va.	....	2	...	2
Charleston . . . . S. C.	36	2	...	38
Key West . . . . . Fla.	78	22	...	100
New Orleans . . . . La.	4006	2049	...	6055
Total . . .	33172	23354	3	56529

II.—AGE.

AGES.	Males.	Females.	Sex not stated.	Total.
Under 5 years of age . . .	3086	3070	. . .	6156
Between 5 years of age and 10	2419	2078	. . .	4497
Between 10 years of age and 15	2337	1940	. . .	4277
Between 15 years of age and 20	4158	3899	. . .	8057
Between 20 years of age and 25	5642	3920	. . .	9562
Between 25 years of age and 30	4962	2737	. . .	7699
Between 30 years of age and 35	2771	1829	. . .	4600
Between 35 years of age and 40	3243	1445	. . .	4688
40 years of age and upward .	3347	1850	. . .	5197
Age not stated	1207	586	3	1796
Total . . .	33172	23354	3	56529

III.—OCCUPATION.

OCCUPATIONS.	Males.	Females.	Sex not stated.	Total.
Merchants	3226	....	...	3226
Mechanics	5155	....	...	5155
Farmers	8031	....	...	8031
Mariners	517	....	...	517
Miners	3	....	...	3
Laborers	5346	....	...	5346
Seamstresses and Milliners	....	361	...	361
Actors	1	....	...	1
Physicians	184	....	...	184
Clergymen	153	....	...	153
Clerks	18	....	...	18
Lawyers	84	....	...	84
Musicians	33	....	...	33
Manufacturers	13	....	...	13
Engineers	26	....	...	26
Artists	46	10	...	56
Teachers	64	3	...	67
Servants	39	374	...	413
Other occupations	128	3	...	131
Not stated	10105	22603	3	32711
Total	33172	23354	3	56529

IV.—COUNTRY WHERE BORN.

COUNTRIES.	Males.	Females.	Sex not stated.	Total.
England	2085	1432	...	3517
Ireland	678	495	...	1173
Scotland	31	10	...	41
Great Britain and Ireland	12522	10847	...	23369
British America	903	599	...	1502
France	1971	1375	...	3346
Spain	112	33	...	145
Portugal	29	3	...	32
Belgium	81	54	...	135
Prussia	1621	1388	...	3009
Switzerland	318	235	...	553
Germany	6703	4729	...	11432
Holland	181	149	...	330
Denmark	20	9	...	29
Norway and Sweden	1019	729	...	1748
Poland	15	2	...	17
Russia	4	2	...	6
Turkey	5	....	...	5
Greece	4	....	...	4
Italy	86	22	...	108
Sicily	3	....	...	3
Sardinia	5	1	...	6
Malta	4	1	...	5
Azores	6	2	...	8
Africa	4	2	...	6
Persia	3	3	...	6
East Indies	2	....	...	2
China	2	1	...	3
Society Islands	....	1	...	1
Sandwich Islands	3	1	...	4
South America	47	15	...	62
Central America	11	1	...	12
Mexico	349	49	...	398
West Indies	695	185	...	880
United States	3103	930	...	4033
Not stated	547	49	3	599
Total	33172	23354	3	56529
Born in the United States	3103	930	...	4033
Aliens	30069	24242	3	52496

Statements exhibiting the *Number and Sex*, *Age*, *Occupation*, and *Country of Birth*, of Passengers arriving in the United States by sea from foreign countries during the year ending September 30, 1844.

I.—ARRIVALS.—Number and Sex.

PORTS AT WHICH THEY ARRIVED.		Males.	Females.	Total.
Passamaquoddy	Me.	2240	1384	3624
Portland and Falmouth	"	14	11	25
Portsmouth	N. H.	129	127	256
Boston and Charlestown	Mass.	4091	2264	6355
Marblehead	"	19	....	19
Fall River	"	17	3	20
Nantucket	"	1	....	1
New Bedford	"	37	8	45
Providence	R. I.	51	82	133
Bristol and Warren	"	7	....	7
Newport	"	9	5	14
New Haven	Ct.	49	9	58
New York City	N. Y.	33951	25811	59762
Philadelphia	Pa.	2458	2428	4886
Wilmington	Del.	22	10	32
Baltimore	Md.	2858	2148	5006
Alexandria	D. C.	19	13	32
Norfolk and Portsmouth	Va.	9	1	10
Richmond	"	118	69	187
Newbern	N. C.	3	2	5
Charleston	S. C.	263	67	330
Key West	Fla.	43	15	58
New Orleans	La.	2489	1410	3899
Total		48897	35867	84764

II.—AGE.

AGES.	Males.	Females.	Total.
Under 5 years of age	3760	3716	7476
Between 5 years of age and 10 . .	3288	3204	6492
Between 10 years of age and 15 . .	2954	2991	5945
Between 15 years of age and 20 . .	5610	6513	12123
Between 20 years of age and 25 . .	10335	7007	17342
Between 25 years of age and 30 . .	8580	4601	13181
Between 30 years of age and 35 . .	4626	2318	6944
Between 35 years of age and 40 . .	3338	1817	5155
40 years of age and upward . . .	5449	3206	8655
Age not stated	957	494	1451
Total	48897	35867	84764

III.—OCCUPATION.

OCCUPATIONS.	Males.	Fe-males.	Total.
Merchants	3960	....	3960
Mechanics	8502	....	8502
Mariners	738	....	738
Farmers	9831	....	9831
Miners	16	....	16
Laborers	9725	....	9725
Seamstresses and Milliners	....	88	88
Actors	13	....	13
Physicians	215	....	215
Clergymen	179	....	179
Clerks	78	....	78
Lawyers	91	....	91
Millers	1	....	1
Musicians	46	....	46
Manufacturers	9	....	9
Artists	93	8	101
Teachers	108	2	110
Bakers	2	....	2
Engineers	40	....	40
Butchers	2	....	2
Servants	42	1132	1174
Other occupations	176	....	176
Not stated	15030	34637	49667
Total	48897	35867	84764

IV.—COUNTRY WHERE BORN.

COUNTRIES.	Males.	Females.	Total.
England	814	543	1357
Ireland	2811	2680	5491
Scotland	13	10	23
Wales	1	2	3
Great Britain and Ireland	21984	18985	40969
British America	1768	943	2711
France	1923	1232	3155
Spain	214	56	270
Portugal	15	1	16
Switzerland	513	326	839
Prussia	872	633	1505
Belgium	112	53	165
Germany	11316	7910	19226
Holland	113	71	184
Denmark	18	7	25
Norway and Sweden	879	432	1311
Poland	27	9	36
Russia	12	1	13
Italy	69	10	79
Greece	3	....	3
Turkey	6	4	10
Malta	2	....	2
Sicily	4	....	4
Sardinia	39	19	58
Corsica	1	....	1
Europe	42	6	48
Asia	2	....	2
East Indies	1	....	1
China	3	....	3
Africa	7	2	9
Liberia	2	3	5
Azores	16	7	23
Cape Verde Islands	1	....	1
South America	46	15	61
Mexico	166	31	197
West Indies	589	182	771
United States	4466	1683	6149
Not stated	27	11	38
Total	48897	35867	84764
Born in the United States	4466	1683	6149
Aliens	44431	34184	78615

Statements exhibiting the *Number and Sex*, *Age*, *Occupation*, and *Country of Birth*, of Passengers arriving in the United States by sea from foreign countries during the year ending September 30, 1845.

I.—ARRIVALS.—Number and Sex.

PORTS AT WHICH THEY ARRIVED.	Males.	Females.	Sex not stated.	Total.
Passamaquoddy . . . . Me.	2241	1687	...	3928
Portland and Falmouth . "	89	33	...	122
Portsmouth . . . . N. H.	9	9	...	18
Boston and Charlestown, Mass.	5391	3484	1406	10281
Marblehead . . . . "	2	1	...	3
Fall River . . . . "	11	9	...	20
Nantucket . . . . "	3	2	...	5
New Bedford . . . "	39	12	...	51
Providence . . . . R. I.	64	69	...	133
Bristol and Warren . "	16	6	...	22
Newport . . . . . "	12	....	...	12
New Haven . . . . . Ct.	8	2	...	10
New York City . . . N. Y.	43432	33082	...	76514
Philadelphia . . . . . Pa.	3025	2742	...	5767
Wilmington . . . . . Del.	14	24	...	38
Baltimore . . . . . . Md.	4128	2903	...	7031
Alexandria . . . . D. C.	6	6	...	12
Charleston . . . . S. C.	243	66	...	309
Key West . . . . . Fla.	65	18	...	83
New Orleans . . . . La.	10381	5156	...	15537
Total . . .	69179	49311	1406	119896

II.—AGE.

AGES.	Males.	Fe-males.	Sex not stated.	Total.
Under 5 years of age . . .	4885	4509	. . .	9394
Between 5 years of age and 10	4413	4126	. . .	8539
Between 10 years of age and 15	4214	4035	. . .	8249
Between 15 years of age and 20	7253	8105	. . .	15358
Between 20 years of age and 25	16018	11033	. . .	27051
Between 25 years of age and 30	12366	6350	. . .	18716
Between 30 years of age and 35	7339	3717	. . .	11056
Between 35 years of age and 40	4784	2483	. . .	7267
40 years of age and upward .	7459	4600	. . .	12059
Age not stated	448	353	1406	2207
Total . . .	69179	49311	1406	119896

III.—OCCUPATION.

OCCUPATIONS.	Males.	Females.	Sex not stated.	Total.
Merchants	5049	....	...	5049
Farmers	19349	....	...	19349
Mechanics	9836	....	...	9836
Mariners	462	....	...	462
Miners	22	....	...	22
Laborers	16552	....	...	16552
Shoemakers	6	....	...	6
Tailors	10	....	...	10
Seamstresses and Milliners	....	103	...	103
Weavers and Spinners	132	143	...	275
Actors and Actresses	34	2	...	36
Clergymen	154	....	...	154
Clerks	57	....	...	57
Physicians	189	....	...	189
Lawyers	80	....	...	80
Manufacturers	13	....	...	13
Musicians	11	....	...	11
Butchers	10	....	...	10
Bakers	6	....	...	6
Painters	1	....	...	1
Printers	3	....	...	3
Engineers	53	....	...	53
Teachers	27	3	...	30
Servants	29	2463	...	2492
Artists	39	3	...	42
Other occupations	215	25	...	240
Not stated	16840	46569	1406	64815
Total	69179	49311	1406	119896

IV.—COUNTRY WHERE BORN.

COUNTRIES.	Males.	Females.	Sex not stated.	Total.
England	1062	598	50	1710
Ireland	3855	3964	822	8641
Scotland	205	154	9	368
Wales	3	8	...	11
Great Britain and Ireland	28598	24702	1	53301
British America	1882	957	356	3195
France	5086	2577	...	7663
Spain	249	55	...	304
Portugal	10	4	...	14
Switzerland	293	178	...	471
Belgium	345	196	...	541
Germany	19911	13227	...	33138
Holland	486	305	...	791
Denmark	29	25	...	54
Prussia	739	478	...	1217
Norway and Sweden	557	371	...	928
Poland	6	....	...	6
Russia	1	....	...	1
Turkey	2	....	1	3
Greece	2	....	...	2
Italy	52	10	1	63
Sicily	5	....	...	5
Sardinia	51	18	...	69
China	6	....	...	6
Africa	3	....	...	3
Algiers	1	....	...	1
Cape Verde Islands	2	....	...	2
Azores	5	....	...	5
South America	70	10	...	80
Central America	14	7	...	21
Mexico	443	55	...	498
West Indies	1036	204	1	1241
United States	4164	1196	165	5525
Not stated	6	12	...	18
Total	69179	49311	1406	119896
Born in the United States	4164	1196	165	5525
Aliens	65015	48115	1241	114371

Statements exhibiting the *Number and Sex, Age, Occupation*, and *Country of Birth*, of Passengers arriving in the United States by sea from foreign countries during the year ending September 30, 1846.

I.—ARRIVALS.—Number and Sex.

PORTS AT WHICH THEY ARRIVED.	Males.	Females.	Sex not stated.	Total.
Passamaquoddy . . . . Me.	3449	2358	...	5807
Portland and Falmouth . "	99	24	...	123
Portsmouth . . . . N. H.	19	6	...	25
Boston and Charlestown, Mass.	7546	5555	897	13998
Fall River . . . . "	34	15	...	49
Nantucket . . . . "	2	....	...	2
New Bedford . . . "	21	9	...	30
Providence . . . . R. I.	37	34	...	71
Bristol and Warren . "	7	1	...	8
Newport . . . . . "	5	4	...	9
New York City . . . N. Y.	56426	42437	...	98863
Philadelphia . . . . . Pa.	3716	3520	...	7236
Wilmington . . . . . Del.	5	1	...	6
Baltimore . . . . . Md.	5546	3791	...	9337
Alexandria . . . . D. C.	31	20	...	51
Norfolk and Portsmouth . Va.	22	9	...	31
Newbern . . . . . N. C.	3	....	...	3
Charleston . . . . S. C.	278	130	...	408
Key West . . . . . Fla.	65	25	...	90
New Orleans . . . . La.	13425	8723	...	22148
Galveston . . . . . Tex.	238	116	...	354
Total . . .	90974	66778	897	158649

II.—AGE.

AGES.	Males.	Fe-males.	Sex not stated.	Total.
Under 5 years of age . . .	6954	6597	. . .	13551
Between 5 years of age and 10	6453	6024	. . .	12477
Between 10 years of age and 15	5482	5368	. . .	10850
Between 15 years of age and 20	9397	10212	. . .	19609
Between 20 years of age and 25	21171	15140	. . .	36311
Between 25 years of age and 30	15837	7997	. . .	23834
Between 30 years of age and 35	9081	5115	. . .	14196
Between 35 years of age and 40	5840	3473	. . .	9313
40 years of age and upward .	10426	6734	. . .	17160
Age not stated	333	118	897	1348
Total . . .	90974	66778	897	158649

III.—OCCUPATION.

OCCUPATIONS.	Males.	Females.	Sex not stated.	Total.
Merchants	4189	....	...	4189
Mechanics	12068	....	...	12068
Mariners	488	....	...	488
Farmers	27944	....	...	27944
Laborers	18193	....	...	18193
Miners	48	....	...	48
Shoemakers	13	....	...	13
Tailors	11	....	...	11
Seamstresses and Milliners	....	21	...	21
Weavers and Spinners	201	97	...	298
Actors and Actresses	2	1	...	3
Physicians	189	....	...	189
Clergymen	164	....	...	164
Clerks	107	....	...	107
Lawyers	102	....	...	102
Masons	6	....	...	6
Printers	2	....	...	2
Teachers	11	4	...	15
Artists	97	14	...	111
Engineers	53	....	...	53
Musicians	8	....	...	8
Manufacturers	126	....	...	126
Painters	2	....	...	2
Butchers	1	....	...	1
Millers	2	....	...	2
Bakers	4	....	...	4
Servants	317	3032	...	3349
Other occupations	498	120	...	618
Not stated	26128	63489	897	90514
Total	90974	66778	897	158649

IV.—COUNTRY WHERE BORN.

COUNTRIES.	Males.	Females.	Sex not stated.	Total.
England	1625	1229	...	2854
Ireland	6388	6561	...	12949
Scotland	192	113	...	305
Wales	82	65	...	147
Great Britain and Ireland	31565	26112	...	57677
British America	2523	1332	...	3855
France	6549	4034	...	10583
Spain	63	10	...	73
Portugal	2	....	...	2
Switzerland	432	266	...	698
Belgium	33	10	...	43
Prussia	351	200	...	551
Germany	33681	23329	...	57010
Holland	575	404	...	979
Denmark	68	46	...	114
Poland	4	....	...	4
Norway and Sweden	1123	793	...	1916
Russia	145	103	...	248
Turkey	4	....	...	4
Italy	70	18	...	88
Greece	3	....	...	3
Sicily	3	1	...	4
Sardinia	50	9	...	59
Malta	4	....	...	4
China	3	4	...	7
East Indies	1	3	...	4
Azores	12	3	...	15
St. Helena	....	3	...	3
Algiers	1	....	...	1
South America	78	14	...	92
Central America	4	1	...	5
Mexico	177	45	...	222
West Indies	1046	305	...	1351
United States	3197	1036	...	4233
Not stated	920	729	897	2546
Total	90974	66778	897	158649
Born in the United States	3197	1036	...	4233
Aliens	87777	65742	897	154416

Statements exhibiting the *Number and Sex*, *Age*, *Occupation*, and *Country of Birth*, of Passengers arriving in the United States by sea from foreign countries during the year ending September 30, 1847.

I.—ARRIVALS.—Number and Sex.

PORTS AT WHICH THEY ARRIVED.	Males.	Females.	Sex not stated.	Total.
Passamaquoddy . . . . Me.	2659	1896	. . .	4555
Waldoboro' . . . . . . "	43	34	. . .	77
Bangor . . . . "	29	30	. . .	59
Portland and Falmouth . "	705	410	. . .	1115
Portsmouth . . . . N. H.	4	3	. . .	7
Boston and Charlestown, Mass.	11900	8328	517	20745
Fall River . . . . "	11	8	. . .	19
New Bedford . . . "	35	31	. . .	66
Edgartown . . . . "	7	6	. . .	13
Nantucket . . . . "	5	. . . .	. . .	5
Providence . . . . R. I.	32	23	. . .	55
Bristol and Warren . "	3	1	. . .	4
Newport . . . . . "	99	50	. . .	149
New London . . . . . . Ct.	43	31	. . .	74
New York City . . . N. Y.	85059	60771	. . .	145830
Philadelphia . . . . . Pa.	7911	6852	14	14777
Baltimore . . . . . . Md.	6968	5050	. . .	12018
Alexandria . . . . . . Va.	127	88	. . .	215
Norfolk and Portsmouth . "	295	186	179	660
Charleston . . . . S. C.	119	45	. . .	164
Savannah. . . . . . . Ga.	4	7	. . .	11
Key West . . . . . . Fla.	102	86	. . .	188
New Orleans . . . . . La.	20784	14019	. . .	34803
Galveston . . . . . . Tex.	2223	1370	208	3873
Total . . .	139167	99325	990	239482

II.—AGE.

AGES.	Males.	Females.	Sex not stated.	Total.
Under 5 years of age . . .	10261	8546	. . .	18807
Between 5 years of age and 10	10050	8176	. . .	18226
Between 10 years of age and 15	11028	9100	. . .	20128
Between 15 years of age and 20	17311	14800	. . .	32111
Between 20 years of age and 25	27471	19099	. . .	46570
Between 25 years of age and 30	23050	13937	. . .	36987
Between 30 years of age and 35	15014	9300	. . .	24314
Between 35 years of age and 40	9990	6655	. . .	16645
40 years of age and upward .	12465	8335	. . .	20800
Age not stated*	2527	1377	990	4894
Total . . .	139167	99325	990	239482

* Of this number—752 males and 490 females were "under 21 years of age;"
1122 males and 656 females were "over 21 years of age."

III.—OCCUPATION.

OCCUPATIONS.	Males.	Females.	Sex not stated.	Total.
Merchants	4218	....	...	4218
Mechanics	24567	....	...	24567
Mariners	409	....	...	409
Farmers	43594	....	...	43594
Miners	13	....	...	13
Laborers	35869	....	...	35869
Seamstresses and Milliners	....	194	...	194
Actors and Actresses	11	3	...	14
Weavers and Spinners	78	37	...	115
Physicians	184	....	...	184
Clergymen	210	....	...	210
Clerks	56	....	...	56
Lawyers	73	....	...	73
Printers	2	....	...	2
Manufacturers	503	....	...	503
Musicians	4	....	...	4
Teachers	17	1	...	18
Millers	1	....	...	1
Artists	182	18	...	200
Engineers	35	....	...	35
Servants	282	2916	...	3198
Other occupations	170	7	...	177
Not stated	28689	96149	990	125828
Total	139167	99325	990	239482

IV.—COUNTRY WHERE BORN.

COUNTRIES.	Males.	Fe-males.	Sex not stated.	Total.
England	2032	1437	7	3476
Ireland	16066	13359	215	29640
Scotland	203	134	...	337
Wales	77	68	...	145
Great Britain and Ireland	54148	41092	...	95240
British America	2413	1414	...	3827
France	12151	7878	11	20040
Spain	95	63	...	158
Portugal	4	1	...	5
Switzerland	116	71	5	192
Belgium	790	683	...	1473
Prussia	493	344	...	837
Germany	43852	29306	286	73444
Holland	1576	1055	...	2631
Denmark	10	2	1	13
Norway and Sweden	738	442	127	1307
Poland	3	5	...	8
Russia	4	....	1	5
Italy	106	54	...	160
Turkey	2	....	...	2
Sicily	3	1	...	4
East Indies	3	5	...	8
China	1	3	...	4
Azores	16	5	...	21
Madeira	2	1	...	3
Sandwich Islands	1	....	...	1
South America	49	21	...	70
Central America	10	11	...	21
Mexico	61	1	...	62
West Indies	990	261	...	1251
United States	3081	1408	25	4514
Not stated	71	200	312	583
Total	139167	99325	990	239482
Born in the United States	3081	1408	25	4514
Aliens	136086	97917	965	234968

Statements exhibiting the *Number and Sex*, *Age*, *Occupation*, and *Country of Birth*, of Passengers arriving in the United States by sea from foreign countries during the year ending September 30, 1848.

I.—ARRIVALS.—Number and Sex.

PORTS AT WHICH THEY ARRIVED.	Males.	Females.	Sex not stated.	Total.
Portland and Falmouth . Me.	1604	1034	...	2638
Passamaquoddy . . . . "	1985	1632	...	3617
Bangor . . . . . . "	....	4	...	4
Portsmouth . . . . N. H.	33	15	...	48
Boston and Charlestown, Mass.	12942	8738	472	22152
Edgartown . . . . "	12	2	...	14
Fall River . . . . "	43	62	...	105
Nantucket . . . . "	5	2	...	7
New Bedford . . . "	50	26	...	76
Bristol and Warren . R. I.	13	2	...	15
Newport . . . . . "	17	9	...	26
Providence . . . . "	31	36	...	67
New London . . . . . Ct.	7	1	...	8
New York City . . . N. Y.	96318	64676	...	160994
Wilmington . . . . . Del.	989	1002	...	1991
Philadelphia . . . . . Pa.	5385	4439	...	9824
Baltimore . . . . . Md.	4133	2958	...	7091
Alexandria . . . . . Va.	24	15	...	39
Norfolk and Portsmouth . "	213	172	...	385
Washington . . . . N. C.	5	4	...	9
Charleston . . . . S. C.	232	104	...	336
Savannah . . . . . . Ga.	27	10	...	37
New Orleans . . . . La.	11614	7685	...	19299
Key West . . . . . Fla.	49	30	...	79
Galveston . . . . . Tex.	397	225	...	622
Total . . .	136128	92883	472	229483

II.—AGE.

AGES.	Males.	Fe-males.	Sex not stated.	Total.
Under 5 years of age . . .	9808	8676	. . .	18484
Between 5 years of age and 10	9215	8034	. . .	17249
Between 10 years of age and 15	9559	7921	. . .	17480
Between 15 years of age and 20	14857	13641	. . .	28498
Between 20 years of age and 25	31198	20469	. . .	51667
Between 25 years of age and 30	23277	12052	. . .	35329
Between 30 years of age and 35	14225	7541	. . .	21766
Between 35 years of age and 40	8815	5073	. . .	13888
40 years of age and upward .	14247	8819	. . .	23066
Age not stated*	927	657	472	2056
Total . . .	136128	92883	472	229483

* Of this number—188, sex not stated, were "under 21 years of age;"
257, sex not stated, were "over 21 years of age."

III.—OCCUPATION.

OCCUPATIONS.	Males.	Females.	Sex not stated.	Total.
Merchants	3407	....	...	3407
Mechanics	23247	....	...	23247
Mariners	352	....	...	352
Miners	127	....	...	127
Farmers	31670	....	...	31670
Laborers	46223	....	...	46223
Shoemakers	2	....	...	2
Tailors	1	....	...	1
Seamstresses and Milliners	....	85	...	85
Actors and Actresses	2	5	...	7
Weavers and Spinners	137	68	...	205
Clergymen	96	....	...	96
Clerks	42	....	...	42
Physicians	138	....	...	138
Lawyers	25	....	...	25
Artists	185	25	...	210
Manufacturers	574	....	...	574
Musicians	26	....	...	26
Masons	1	....	...	1
Printers	3	....	...	3
Engineers	66	....	...	66
Teachers	14	1	...	15
Servants	95	4338	...	4433
Other occupations	152	4	...	156
Not stated	29543	88357	472	118372
Total	136128	92883	472	229483

IV.—COUNTRY WHERE BORN.

COUNTRIES.	Males.	Females.	Sex not stated.	Total.
England	2664	1791	...	4455
Ireland	13444	11358	...	24802
Scotland	404	255	...	659
Wales	214	134	...	348
Great Britain and Ireland	68595	49234	...	117829
British America	4006	2467	...	6473
France	4850	2893	...	7743
Spain	136	28	...	164
Portugal	50	17	...	67
Switzerland	198	121	...	319
Belgium	534	363	...	897
Prussia	269	182	...	451
Germany	35963	22051	...	58014
Holland	534	384	...	918
Denmark	144	66	...	210
Norway and Sweden	580	323	...	903
Russia	....	1	...	1
Turkey	3	....	...	3
Italy	155	64	...	219
Greece	1	....	...	1
Sicily	20	2	...	22
East Indies	4	2	...	6
Azores	10	10	...	20
Africa	5	5	...	10
Asia	2	....	...	2
South America	106	44	...	150
Central America	4	....	...	4
Sandwich Islands	2	1	...	3
Mexico	21	3	...	24
West Indies	988	350	...	1338
United States	2222	734	...	2956
Not stated	....	....	472	472
Total	136128	92883	472	229483
Born in the United States	2222	734	...	2956
Aliens	133906	92149	472	226527

Statements exhibiting the *Number and Sex*, *Age*, *Occupation*, and *Country of Birth*, of Passengers arriving in the United States by sea from foreign countries during the year ending September 30, 1849.

I.—ARRIVALS.—Number and Sex.

PORTS AT WHICH THEY ARRIVED.	Males.	Females.	Sex not stated.	Total.
Portland and Falmouth . Me.	1232	958	70	2260
Passamaquoddy . . . . "	1511	1071	...	2582
Penobscot . . . . . "	1	2	...	3
Portsmouth . . . . N. H.	88	54	...	142
Boston and Charlestown, Mass.	16830	12416	244	29490
Edgartown . . . . "	72	66	...	138
Marblehead . . . . "	16	1	...	17
Fall River . . . . "	39	56	...	95
Nantucket . . . . "	7	5	...	12
New Bedford . . . "	19	12	...	31
Bristol and Warren . R. I.	17	2	2	21
Newport . . . . . "	9	9	...	18
Providence . . . . "	37	34	...	71
New York City . . . N. Y.	128954	84782	...	213736
Philadelphia . . . . . Pa.	8026	7443	42	15511
Baltimore . . . . . Md.	4849	3223	...	8072
Alexandria . . . . . Va.	12	11	...	23
Norfolk and Portsmouth . "	212	137	...	349
Charleston . . . . S. C.	710	237	61	1008
Savannah . . . . . . Ga.	110	99	...	209
Key West . . . . . Fla.	41	34	...	75
Mobile . . . . Ala.	112	60	...	172
New Orleans . . . . La.	16072	9137	...	25209
Galveston . . . . . Tex.	280	66	93	439
Total . . .	179256	119915	512	299683

II.—AGE.

AGES.	Males.	Females.	Sex not stated.	Total.
Under 5 years of age . . .	12808	11157	...	23965
Between 5 years of age and 10	11309	10153	...	21462
Between 10 years of age and 15	11598	10306	...	21904
Between 15 years of age and 20	20495	18039	...	38534
Between 20 years of age and 25	43180	27542	...	70722
Between 25 years of age and 30	30864	14981	...	45845
Between 30 years of age and 35	19491	10055	...	29546
Between 35 years of age and 40	10546	5706	...	16252
40 years of age and upward .	18785	11894	...	30679
Age not stated	180	82	512	774
Total . . .	179256	119915	512	299683

III.—OCCUPATION.

OCCUPATIONS.	Males.	Females.	Sex not stated.	Total.
Merchants	3508	....	...	3508
Mechanics	29564	....	...	29564
Mariners	625	....	...	625
Farmers	39675	....	...	39675
Laborers	62179	....	...	62179
Miners	509	....	...	509
Shoemakers	8	....	...	8
Tailors	5	....	...	5
Seamstresses and Milliners	....	187	...	187
Weavers and Spinners	225	80	...	305
Actors and Actresses	8	5	...	13
Physicians	238	....	...	238
Lawyers	178	....	...	178
Clergymen	172	....	...	172
Clerks	263	....	...	263
Hatters	1	....	...	1
Butchers	8	....	...	8
Bakers	1	....	...	1
Millers	15	....	...	15
Artists	192	8	...	200
Engineers	142	....	...	142
Musicians	8	2	...	10
Teachers	88	73	...	161
Manufacturers	382	....	...	382
Masons	6	....	...	6
Servants	458	3213	...	3671
Other occupations	522	73	...	595
Not stated	40276	116274	512	157062
Total	179256	119915	512	299683

IV.—COUNTRY WHERE BORN.

COUNTRIES.	Males.	Females.	Sex not stated.	Total.
England	3385	2651	...	6036
Ireland	16605	14716	...	31321
Scotland	619	441	...	1060
Wales	154	118	...	272
Great Britain and Ireland	101447	74394	...	175841
British America	4283	2537	70	6890
France	3878	1963	...	5841
Spain	227	102	...	329
Portugal	18	8	...	26
Switzerland	10	3	...	13
Belgium	330	260	...	590
Prussia	135	38	...	173
Germany	40568	19494	...	60062
Holland	711	479	...	1190
Denmark	7	1	...	8
Norway and Sweden	2168	1305	...	3473
Poland	4	....	...	4
Russia	29	15	...	44
Italy	157	51	...	208
Sicily	1	....	...	1
Turkey	9	....	...	9
China	3	....	...	3
East Indies	6	2	...	8
Azores	35	13	...	48
Isle of France	1	....	...	1
Morocco	1	....	...	1
Africa	2	....	...	2
South America	150	40	...	190
Mexico	488	30	...	518
West Indies	764	309	...	1073
Central America	233	....	...	233
United States	2024	635	...	2659
Not stated	804	310	442	1556
Total	179256	119915	512	299683
Born in the United States	2024	635	...	2659
Aliens	177232	119280	512	297024

Statements exhibiting the *Number and Sex*, *Age*, *Occupation*, and *Country of Birth*, of Passengers arriving in the United States by sea from foreign countries during the year ending September 30, 1850.

I.—ARRIVALS.—Number and Sex.

PORTS AT WHICH THEY ARRIVED.	Males.	Females.	Sex not stated.	Total.
Portland and Falmouth . Me.	1222	701	235	2158
Passamaquoddy . . . . "	1214	876	...	2090
Portsmouth . . . . N. H.	53	13	...	66
Boston and Charlestown, Mass.	14349	12026	237	26612
Marblehead . . . . "	38	10	...	48
Fall River . . . . "	16	13	...	29
New Bedford . . . "	117	28	1	146
Bristol and Warren . R. I.	24	3	...	27
Providence . . . . "	53	63	...	116
Newport . . . . . "	24	....	...	24
New York City . . . N. Y.	107866	77016	...	184882
Philadelphia . . . . . Pa.	5259	5256	...	10515
Baltimore . . . . . Md.	4406	3178	...	7584
Alexandria . . . . . Va.	14	3	...	17
Norfolk and Portsmouth . "	13	4	...	17
Charleston . . . . S. C.	1177	440	...	1617
Savannah. . . . . . Ga.	90	61	...	151
Key West . . . . . Fla.	70	63	...	133
Mobile . . . . Ala.	278	53	282	613
New Orleans . . . . La.	22101	11979	...	34080
Galveston . . . . . Tex.	393	118	283	794
San Francisco . . . . Cal.	42127	1488	...	43615
Total . . .	200904	113392	1038	315334

II.—AGE.

AGES.	Males.	Females.	Sex not stated.	Total.
Under 5 years of age . . .	11426	8883	. . .	20309
Between 5 years of age and 10	10759	8805	. . .	19564
Between 10 years of age and 15	12384	10286	. . .	22670
Between 15 years of age and 20	18923	16917	. . .	35840
Between 20 years of age and 25	33033	23594	. . .	56627
Between 25 years of age and 30	26296	14957	. . .	41253
Between 30 years of age and 35	18529	10965	. . .	29494
Between 35 years of age and 40	11618	6636	. . .	18254
40 years of age and upward .	15396	10689	. . .	26085
Age not stated	42540	1660	1038	45238
Total . . .	200904	113392	1038	315334

III.—OCCUPATION.

OCCUPATIONS.	Males.	Females.	Sex not stated.	Total.
Merchants	6400	....	...	6400
Farmers	42873	....	...	42873
Mechanics	23378	....	...	23378
Mariners	1089	....	...	1089
Miners	937	....	...	937
Laborers	46640	....	...	46640
Shoemakers	19	....	...	19
Tailors	16	....	...	16
Seamstresses and Milliners	....	320	...	320
Weavers and Spinners	60	31	...	91
Actors and Actresses	73	25	...	98
Physicians	236	....	...	236
Lawyers	30	....	...	30
Clergymen	72	....	...	72
Clerks	203	....	...	203
Masons	6	....	...	6
Musicians	40	10	...	50
Manufacturers	134	....	...	134
Butchers	14	....	...	14
Bakers	13	....	...	13
Artists	111	25	...	136
Engineers	136	....	...	136
Teachers	69	227	...	296
Millers	8	....	...	8
Printers	1	....	...	1
Painters	4	....	...	4
Servants	613	2590	...	3203
Other occupations	220	11	...	231
Not stated	77509	110153	1038	188700
Total	200904	113392	1038	315334

IV.—COUNTRY WHERE BORN.

COUNTRIES.	Males.	Females.	Sex not stated.	Total.
England	2959	2316	1	5276
Ireland	13463	14211	...	27674
Scotland	357	270	...	627
Wales	29	20	...	49
Great Britain and Ireland	80173	61686	...	141859
British America	4824	2738	234	7796
France	5521	2488	...	8009
Spain	269	56	...	325
Portugal	176	190	...	366
Switzerland	104	42	...	146
Belgium	530	525	...	1055
Prussia	12	2	...	14
Germany	39206	23962	...	63168
Denmark	9	1	...	10
Holland	399	177	...	576
Norway and Sweden	819	544	...	1363
Poland	2	1	...	3
Russia	18	13	...	31
Turkey	13	....	...	13
Greece	2	....	...	2
Italy	289	71	...	360
Sicily	8	2	...	10
Sardinia	3	....	...	3
China	2	1	...	3
East Indies	3	1	...	4
Azores	174	6	...	180
Sandwich Islands	10	7	...	17
South America	1726	736	...	2462
Central America	57	14	...	71
Mexico	415	83	...	498
West Indies	2100	803	...	2903
United States	4573	757	...	5330
Not stated	42659	1669	803	45131
Total	200904	113392	1038	315334
Born in the United States	4573	757	...	5330
Aliens	196331	112635	1038	310004

Statements exhibiting the *Number and Sex*, *Age*, *Occupation*, and *Country of Birth*, of Passengers arriving in the United States by sea from foreign countries during the quarter ending December 31, 1850.

I.—ARRIVALS.—Number and Sex.

PORTS AT WHICH THEY ARRIVED.	Males.	Females.	Sex not stated.	Total.
Portland and Falmouth . Me.	140	79	179	398
Passamaquoddy . . . . "	432	207	...	639
Portsmouth . . . . N. H.	3	2	...	5
Boston and Charlestown, Mass.	2504	2385	2	4891
Marblehead . . . . "	2	1	...	3
New Bedford . . . "	....	10	...	10
Fall River . . . . "	1	5	...	6
Providence . . . . R. I.	12	14	...	26
Newport . . . . . "	5	3	...	8
New York City . . . N. Y.	21457	15374	...	36831
Philadelphia . . . . . Pa.	1578	1620	...	3198
Baltimore . . . . . . Md.	859	784	...	1643
Alexandria . . . . . . Va.	14	10	...	24
Savannah. . . . . . . Ga.	136	84	...	220
Key West . . . . . . Fla.	35	17	...	52
Mobile . . . . Ala.	74	41	...	115
New Orleans . . . . . La.	10734	6255	...	16989
Galveston . . . . . . Tex.	296	216	...	512
Total . . .	38282	27107	181	65570

II.—AGE.

AGES.	Males.*	Females.	Sex not stated.	Total.
Under 5 years of age . . .	2289	2394	...	4683
Between 5 years of age and 10	2166	2271	...	4437
Between 10 years of age and 15	2452	2253	...	4705
Between 15 years of age and 20	3454	4011	...	7465
Between 20 years of age and 25	7273	4878	...	12151
Between 25 years of age and 30	6552	3579	...	10131
Between 30 years of age and 35	5474	2854	...	8328
Between 35 years of age and 40	3622	2002	...	5624
40 years of age and upward .	4856	2765	...	7621
Age not stated	144	100	181	425
Total . . .	38282	27107	181	65570

III.—OCCUPATION.

OCCUPATIONS.	Males.	Females.	Sex not stated.	Total.
Merchants	2188	....	...	2188
Farmers	8604	....	...	8604
Mechanics	5131	....	...	5131
Mariners	142	....	...	142
Miners	10	....	...	10
Laborers	13128	....	...	13128
Shoemakers	7	....	...	7
Tailors	8	....	...	8
Seamstresses and Milliners	....	46	...	46
Weavers and Spinners	12	1	...	13
Physicians	78	....	...	78
Lawyers	17	....	...	17
Clergymen	29	....	...	29
Clerks	54	....	...	54
Engineers	25	....	...	25
Millers	3	....	...	3
Manufacturers	27	....	...	27
Musicians	1	....	...	1
Teachers	14	2	...	16
Butchers	5	....	...	5
Artists	21	6	...	27
Painters	1	....	...	1
Printers	1	....	...	1
Masons	3	....	...	3
Bakers	1	....	...	1
Servants	45	373	...	418
Other occupations	83	....	...	83
Not stated	8644	26679	181	35504
Total	38282	27107	181	65570

IV.—COUNTRY WHERE BORN.

COUNTRIES.	Males.	Females.	Sex not stated.	Total.
England	912	609	...	1521
Ireland	6411	6095	...	12506
Scotland	145	88	...	233
Wales	81	112	...	193
Great Britain and Ireland	13189	11962	...	25151
British America	957	623	...	1580
France	952	420	...	1372
Spain	90	14	...	104
Switzerland	106	73	...	179
Belgium	5	20	...	25
Germany	8703	6266	...	14969
Prussia	461	284	...	745
Holland	79	29	...	108
Denmark	7	3	...	10
Norway and Sweden	146	60	...	206
Poland	2	....	...	2
Turkey	2	....	...	2
Italy	25	21	...	46
Sardinia	3	....	...	3
Sicily	4	5	...	9
Europe	3	....	...	3
South America	81	10	...	91
Mexico	97	2	...	99
West Indies	204	64	...	268
United States	5292	302	...	5594
Not stated	325	45	181	551
Total	38282	27107	181	65570
Born in the United States	5292	302	...	5594
Aliens	32990	26805	181	59976

Statements exhibiting the *Number and Sex*, *Age*, *Occupation*, and *Country of Birth*, of Passengers arriving in the United States by sea from foreign countries during the year ending December 31, 1851.

I.—ARRIVALS.—Number and Sex.

PORTS AT WHICH THEY ARRIVED.	Males.	Females.	Sex not stated.	Total.
Portland and Falmouth . Me.	1468	914	42	2424
Passamaquoddy . . . . "	1726	1181	. . .	2907
Penobscot . . . . . . "	4	4	. . .	8
Belfast . . . . "	12	13	. . .	25
Portsmouth . . . . N. H.	62	46	. . .	108
Boston and Charlestown, Mass.	13903	11267	17	25187
Marblehead . . . . "	57	49	. . .	106
New Bedford . . . "	42	11	. . .	53
Fall River . . . . "	14	18	. . .	32
Nantucket . . . . "	134	85	. . .	219
Providence . . . . R. I.	30	40	. . .	70
Bristol and Warren . "	4	. . . .	. . .	4
Newport . . . . . . "	59	42	. . .	101
New York City . . . N. Y.	174914	119531	. . .	294445
Philadelphia . . . . . Pa.	9803	8753	. . .	18556
Baltimore . . . . . . Md.	5002	3587	. . .	8589
Alexandria . . . . . . Va.	15	14	. . .	29
Charleston . . . . S. C.	1212	594	5	1811
Savannah. . . . . . . Ga.	304	206	. . .	510
Key West . . . . . . Fla.	44	37	. . .	81
Mobile . . . . Ala.	207	135	2	344
New Orleans . . . . . La.	35302	16709	. . .	52011
Galveston . . . . . . Tex.	699	509	. . .	1208
Total . . .	245017	163745	66	408828

II.—AGE.

AGES.	Males.	Females.	Sex not stated.	Total.
Under 5 years of age . . .	15425	14644	. . .	30069
Between 5 years of age and 10	15319	14321	. . .	29640
Between 10 years of age and 15	15543	13989	. . .	29532
Between 15 years of age and 20	27382	25151	. . .	52533
Between 20 years of age and 25	55590	38631	. . .	94221
Between 25 years of age and 30	42734	19824	. . .	62558
Between 30 years of age and 35	28656	13613	. . .	42269
Between 35 years of age and 40	16138	6640	. . .	22778
40 years of age and upward .	27559	16513	. . .	44072
Age not stated	671	419	66	1156
Total . . .	245017	163745	66	408828

III.—OCCUPATION.

OCCUPATIONS.	Males.	Females.	Sex not stated.	Total.
Merchants	12795	....	...	12795
Farmers	50491	....	...	50491
Mechanics	26483	....	...	26483
Mariners	813	....	...	813
Miners	2605	....	...	2605
Laborers	88848	....	...	88848
Shoemakers	20	....	...	20
Tailors	34	....	...	34
Seamstresses and Milliners	....	309	...	309
Weavers and Spinners	39	6	...	45
Physicians	282	....	...	282
Lawyers	106	....	...	106
Clergymen	129	....	...	129
Clerks	107	....	...	107
Musicians	36	12	...	48
Manufacturers	161	....	...	161
Millers	34	....	...	34
Teachers	21	3	...	24
Engineers	103	....	...	103
Butchers	39	....	...	39
Artists	179	2	...	181
Hatters	3	....	...	3
Painters	5	....	...	5
Printers	1	....	...	1
Bakers	40	....	...	40
Masons	18	....	...	18
Servants	33	3282	...	3315
Other occupations	462	10	...	472
Not stated	61130	160121	66	221317
Total	245017	163745	66	408828

IV.—COUNTRY WHERE BORN.

COUNTRIES.	Males.	Females.	Sex not stated.	Total.
England	3174	2130	2	5306
Ireland	29287	26587	...	55874
Scotland	579	387	...	966
Wales	149	62	...	211
Great Britain and Ireland	117482	92901	...	210383
British America	4780	2658	...	7438
France	12801	7325	...	20126
Spain	362	73	...	435
Portugal	34	16	...	50
Switzerland	284	143	...	427
Prussia	723	437	...	1160
Germany	43487	27835	...	71322
Holland	276	76	...	352
Denmark	13	1	...	14
Norway and Sweden	1448	976	...	2424
Poland	9	1	...	10
Russia	1	....	...	1
Turkey	2	....	...	2
Italy	327	96	...	423
Sicily	20	4	...	24
East Indies	1	1	...	2
Azores	77	26	...	103
St. Helena	1	1	...	2
Africa	3	....	...	3
Madeira	8	....	...	8
South America	41	18	...	59
Central America	96	....	...	96
Mexico	175	6	...	181
West Indies	1491	438	...	1929
United States	27836	1526	...	29362
Not stated	50	21	64	135
Total	245017	163745	66	408828
Born in the United States	27836	1526	...	29362
Aliens	217181	162219	66	379466

Statements exhibiting the *Number and Sex*, *Age*, *Occupation*, and *Country of Birth*, of Passengers arriving in the United States by sea from foreign countries during the year ending December 31, 1852.

I.—ARRIVALS.—Number and Sex.

PORTS AT WHICH THEY ARRIVED.	Males.	Females.	Sex not stated.	Total.
Portland and Falmouth . Me.	753	388	1	1142
Passamaquoddy . . . . "	1070	533	...	1603
Portsmouth . . . . N. H.	33	6	...	39
Boston and Charlestown, Mass.	12073	9758	...	21831
Marblehead . . . . "	38	14	...	52
Fall River . . . . "	59	45	...	104
Nantucket . . . . "	1	....	...	1
New Bedford . . . "	54	10	...	64
Bristol and Warren . R. I.	12	1	...	13
Providence . . . . "	25	11	...	36
Newport . . . . . "	3	2	...	5
New York City . . . N. Y.	180112	123041	...	303153
Philadelphia . . . . . Pa.	9558	8401	...	17959
Baltimore . . . . . Md.	8185	5963	...	14148
Alexandria . . . . . Va.	1	7	...	8
Charleston . . . . S. C.	1017	500	...	1517
Savannah. . . . . . Ga.	219	153	25	397
Key West . . . . . Fla.	34	36	...	70
Mobile . . . . . . Ala.	208	91	...	299
New Orleans . . . . La.	21088	11214	...	32302
Galveston . . . . . Tex.	1188	....	1412	2600
Total . . .	235731	160174	1438	397343

II.—AGE.

AGES.	Males.	Females.	Sex not stated.	Total.
Under 5 years of age . . .	15598	15386	...	30984
Between 5 years of age and 10	16149	15144	...	31293
Between 10 years of age and 15	14648	13349	...	27997
Between 15 years of age and 20	28027	23960	...	51987
Between 20 years of age and 25	37222	35373	...	72595
Between 25 years of age and 30	40690	19786	...	60476
Between 30 years of age and 35	26264	12763	...	39027
Between 35 years of age and 40	14828	7163	...	21991
40 years of age and upward .	26469	16925	...	43394
Age not stated	15836	325	1438	17599
Total . . .	235731	160174	1438	397343

III.—OCCUPATION.

OCCUPATIONS.	Males.	Females.	Sex not stated.	Total.
Merchants	11502	....	...	11502
Farmers	58023	....	...	58023
Mechanics	24120	....	...	24120
Mariners	1037	....	...	1037
Miners	1300	....	...	1300
Laborers	75267	....	...	75267
Shoemakers	25	....	...	25
Tailors	63	....	...	63
Seamstresses and Milliners	....	156	...	156
Weavers and Spinners	69	35	...	104
Actors and Actresses	2	3	...	5
Physicians	263	....	...	263
Lawyers	19	....	...	19
Clergymen	107	....	...	107
Clerks	131	....	...	131
Engineers	91	....	...	91
Teachers	23	4	...	27
Artists	130	4	...	134
Butchers	20	....	...	20
Manufacturers	122	....	...	122
Musicians	17	....	...	17
Millers	7	....	...	7
Servants	55	887	...	942
Other occupations	258	12	...	270
Not stated	63080	159073	1438	223591
Total	235731	160174	1438	397343

IV.—COUNTRY WHERE BORN.

COUNTRIES.	Males.	Females.	Sex not stated.	Total.
England	17307	12700	...	30007
Ireland	85715	73808	25	159548
Scotland	4733	3415	...	8148
Wales	432	309	...	741
Great Britain and Ireland	1050	753	...	1803
British America	4091	2261	...	6352
France	4292	2471	...	6763
Spain	310	81	...	391
Portugal	60	8	...	68
Switzerland	1786	1002	...	2788
Prussia	1414	929	...	2343
Belgium	4	4	...	8
Germany	85486	56677	1412	143575
Holland	983	736	...	1719
Denmark	3	....	...	3
Norway and Sweden	2440	1663	...	4103
Russia	2	....	...	2
Poland	101	9	...	110
Turkey	3	....	...	3
Greece	7	3	...	10
Italy	257	40	...	297
Sicily	37	7	...	44
Sardinia	10	....	...	10
Europe	290	183	...	473
East Indies	2	2	...	4
St. Helena	....	4	...	4
Azores	131	47	...	178
South America	26	13	...	39
Mexico	65	7	...	72
West Indies	850	382	...	1232
United States	23262	2478	...	25740
Not stated	582	182	1	765
Total	235731	160174	1438	397343
Born in the United States	23262	2478	...	25740
Aliens	212469	157696	1438	371603

Statements exhibiting the *Number and Sex*, *Age*, *Occupation*, and *Country of Birth*, of Passengers arriving in the United States by sea from foreign countries during the year ending December 31, 1853.

I.—ARRIVALS.—Number and Sex.

PORTS AT WHICH THEY ARRIVED.	Males.	Females.	Sex not stated.	Total.
Portland and Falmouth . Me.	324	193	...	517
Passamaquoddy . . . . "	1794	448	45	2287
Portsmouth . . . . N. H.	11	16	...	27
Boston and Charlestown, Mass.	13936	11875	21	25832
Marblehead . . . . "	9	9	...	18
Fall River . . . . "	4	7	...	11
New Bedford . . . "	47	15	2	64
Edgartown . . . . "	4	....	...	4
Bristol and Warren . R. I.	3	....	...	3
Providence . . . . "	30	46	4	80
Newport . . . . . "	1	....	...	1
New York City . . . N. Y.	175190	119628	...	294818
Philadelphia . . . . . Pa.	10122	9089	...	19211
Baltimore . . . . . Md.	6369	4999	...	11368
Norfolk and Portsmouth . Va.	207	1	...	208
Charleston . . . . S. C.	762	307	...	1069
Savannah . . . . . . Ga.	29	13	...	42
Key West . . . . . . Fla.	61	32	...	93
Mobile . . . . Ala.	148	61	...	209
New Orleans . . . . . La.	26487	16541	...	43028
Galveston . . . . . . Tex.	1187	894	...	2081
Astoria . . . . . . Oregon	7	4	...	11
Total . . .	236732	164178	72	400982

II.—AGE.

AGES.	Males.	Females.	Sex not stated.	Total.
Under 5 years of age . . .	14548	14410	. . .	28958
Between 5 years of age and 10	15432	14850	. . .	30282
Between 10 years of age and 15	14638	13453	. . .	28091
Between 15 years of age and 20	30473	26384	. . .	56857
Between 20 years of age and 25	52225	37033	. . .	89258
Between 25 years of age and 30	40032	19780	. . .	59812
Between 30 years of age and 35	26653	13416	. . .	40069
Between 35 years of age and 40	14775	7105	. . .	21880
40 years of age and upward .	27046	17512	. . .	44558
Age not stated	910	235	72	1217
Total . . .	236732	164178	72	400982

III.—OCCUPATION.

OCCUPATIONS.	Males.	Females.	Sex not stated.	Total.
Merchants	12782	....	...	12782
Farmers	56322	....	...	56322
Mechanics	16661	....	...	16661
Mariners	983	....	...	983
Miners	1837	....	...	1837
Laborers	83022	....	...	83022
Shoemakers	89	....	...	89
Tailors	101	....	...	101
Seamstresses and Milliners	....	216	...	216
Weavers and Spinners	77	14	...	91
Actors and Actresses	25	12	...	37
Physicians	238	....	...	238
Lawyers	93	....	...	93
Clergymen	133	....	...	133
Clerks	154	....	...	154
Hatters	1	....	...	1
Masons	11	....	...	11
Manufacturers	298	....	...	298
Musicians	25	....	...	25
Teachers	16	1	...	17
Engineers	274	....	...	274
Printers	1	....	...	1
Painters	6	....	...	6
Butchers	26	....	...	26
Bakers	8	....	...	8
Millers	49	....	...	49
Artists	164	15	...	179
Servants	37	3901	...	3938
Other occupations	319	1	...	320
Not stated	62980	160018	72	223070
Total	236732	164178	72	400982

IV.—COUNTRY WHERE BORN.

COUNTRIES.	Males.	Females.	Sex not stated.	Total.
England	16075	12792	...	28867
Ireland	86353	76296	...	162649
Scotland	3234	2772	...	6006
Wales	143	79	...	222
Great Britain and Ireland	1401	1080	...	2481
British America	3364	2060	...	5424
France	6729	4041	...	10770
Spain	862	229	...	1091
Portugal	66	29	...	95
Switzerland	1638	1110	...	2748
Germany	83520	57133	...	140653
Belgium	73	14	...	87
Prussia	697	596	...	1293
Holland	372	228	...	600
Denmark	29	3	...	32
Norway and Sweden	1891	1473	...	3364
Poland	24	9	...	33
Russia	3	....	...	3
Turkey	15	....	...	15
Greece	9	3	...	12
Italy	203	64	...	267
Sicily	46	10	...	56
Sardinia	151	81	...	232
China	42	....	...	42
East Indies	2	3	...	5
Azores	153	56	...	209
Madeira	23	32	...	55
Africa	6	2	...	8
South America	23	15	...	38
Mexico	136	26	...	162
West Indies	267	139	...	406
United States	28774	3563	...	32337
Not stated	408	240	72	720
Total	236732	164178	72	400982
Born in the United States	28774	3563	...	32337
Aliens	207958	160615	72	368645

Statements exhibiting the *Number and Sex*, *Age*, *Occupation*, and *Country of Birth*, of Passengers arriving in the United States by sea from foreign countries during the year ending December 31, 1854.

I.—ARRIVALS.—Number and Sex.

PORTS AT WHICH THEY ARRIVED.		Males.	Females.	Total.
Portland and Falmouth	Me.	1271	586	1857
Passamaquoddy	"	3354	898	4252
Portsmouth	N. H.	9	4	13
Boston and Charlestown	Mass.	15113	12370	27483
Nantucket	"	4	....	4
Marblehead	"	4	5	9
Fall River	"	4	1	5
Edgartown	"	105	77	182
New Bedford	"	68	14	82
Bristol and Warren	R. I.	3	....	3
Newport	"	11	19	30
Providence	"	28	33	61
New York City	N. Y.	201580	126396	327976
Philadelphia	Pa.	8384	6648	15032
Baltimore	Md.	6995	6159	13154
Alexandria	Va.	21	11	32
Norfolk and Portsmouth	"	9	3	12
Newbern	N. C.	4	3	7
Charleston	S. C.	812	321	1133
Key West	Fla.	145	97	242
Mobile	Ala.	145	46	191
New Orleans	La.	31507	19662	51169
Galveston	Tex.	1782	1276	3058
San Francisco	Cal.	13529	958	14487
Total		284887	175587	460474

II.—AGE.

AGES.	Males.	Females.	Total.
Under 5 years of age	18789	17692	36481
Between 5 years of age and 10 . .	17920	16406	34326
Between 10 years of age and 15 . .	15589	13617	29206
Between 15 years of age and 20 . .	43841	32033	75874
Between 20 years of age and 25 . .	56441	32807	89248
Between 25 years of age and 30 . .	51940	22824	74764
Between 30 years of age and 35 . .	30028	12376	42404
Between 35 years of age and 40 . .	20555	9456	30011
40 years of age and upward . . .	29476	17901	47377
Age not stated	308	475	783
Total	284887	175587	460474

III.—OCCUPATION.

OCCUPATIONS.	Males.	Females.	Total.
Merchants	15173	....	15173
Farmers	87188	....	87188
Mechanics	31470	....	31470
Mariners	1260	....	1260
Miners	2155	....	2155
Laborers	82373	....	82373
Shoemakers	157	....	157
Tailors	108	....	108
Seamstresses and Milliners	....	183	183
Weavers and Spinners	76	220	296
Actors	13	....	13
Physicians	237	....	237
Lawyers	135	....	135
Clergymen	139	....	139
Clerks	158	....	158
Engineers	213	....	213
Artists	66	1	67
Teachers	52	2	54
Manufacturers	364	....	364
Printers	4	....	4
Painters	11	....	11
Masons	11	....	11
Millers	53	....	53
Musicians	50	4	54
Butchers	4	....	4
Bakers	21	....	21
Servants	47	3310	3357
Other occupations	981	59	1040
Not stated	62368	171808	234176
Total	284887	175587	460474

IV.—COUNTRY WHERE BORN.

COUNTRIES.	Males.	Females.	Total.
England	28989	19912	48901
Ireland	56516	45090	101606
Scotland	2477	2128	4605
Wales	483	333	816
Great Britain and Ireland	2577	1748	4325
British America	4532	2359	6891
France	8812	4505	13317
Spain	1097	336	1433
Portugal	64	8	72
Switzerland	4802	3151	7953
Prussia	5350	3605	8955
Belgium	193	73	266
Germany	121766	84288	206054
Holland	885	649	1534
Denmark	407	284	691
Norway and Sweden	2057	1474	3531
Poland	117	91	208
Russia	2	....	2
Turkey	7	....	7
Greece	1	....	1
Italy	681	303	984
Sardinia	140	79	219
Sicily	40	20	60
Malta	2	....	2
China	12427	673	13100
Australia	11	....	11
Azores	214	40	254
Madeira	9	5	14
St. Helena	1	2	3
Society Islands	1	2	3
Sandwich Islands	11	6	17
South America	79	57	136
Central America	21	3	24
Mexico	363	83	446
West Indies	746	290	1036
United States	28710	3931	32641
Not stated	297	59	356
Total	284887	175587	460474
Born in the United States	28710	3931	32641
Aliens	256177	171656	427833

Statements exhibiting the *Number and Sex*, *Age*, *Occupation*, and *Country of Birth*, of Passengers arriving in the United States by sea from foreign countries during the year ending December 31, 1855.

I.—ARRIVALS.—Number and Sex.

PORTS AT WHICH THEY ARRIVED.	Males.	Females.	Sex not stated.	Total.
Portland and Falmouth . Me.	166	155	...	321
Passamaquoddy . . . . "	1981	694	...	2675
Portsmouth . . . . N. H.	17	4	...	21
Boston and Charlestown, Mass.	10261	7474	...	17735
Fall River . . . . "	1	....	...	1
Edgartown . . . . "	28	6	...	34
New Bedford . . . "	142	59	...	201
Salem . . . . "	2	....	...	2
Bristol and Warren . R. I.	9	1	...	10
Providence . . . . "	39	27	...	66
Newport . . . . . . "	4	3	...	7
Oswego . . . . . . N. Y.	4041	1031	...	5072
New York City . . . "	97724	63766	...	161490
Philadelphia . . . . . . Pa.	3909	3672	...	7581
Baltimore . . . . . . Md.	3692	3138	...	6830
Alexandria . . . . . . Va.	1	2	...	3
Norfolk and Portsmouth . "	2	1	...	3
Newbern . . . . . . N. C.	3	4	...	7
Charleston . . . . S. C.	555	205	12	772
Key West . . . . . . Fla.	142	77	...	219
Mobile . . . . Ala.	97	69	...	166
New Orleans . . . . . La.	11741	8647	...	20388
Galveston . . . . . . Tex.	1126	922	...	2048
La Salle . . . . "	41	33	...	74
San Francisco . . . . . Cal.	4457	293	...	4750
Total . . .	140181	90283	12	230476

II.—AGE.

AGES.	Males.	Females.	Sex not stated.	Total.
Under 5 years of age . . .	10117	9819	. . .	19936
Between 5 years of age and 10	9200	8833	. . .	18033
Between 10 years of age and 15	8005	7071	. . .	15076
Between 15 years of age and 20	20008	17302	. . .	37310
Between 20 years of age and 25	24154	15413	. . .	39567
Between 25 years of age and 30	24030	10798	. . .	34828
Between 30 years of age and 35	15609	6099	. . .	21708
Between 35 years of age and 40	12777	5250	. . .	18027
40 years of age and upward .	15874	9281	. . .	25155
Age not stated	407	417	12	836
Total . . .	140181	90283	12	230476

III.—OCCUPATION.

OCCUPATIONS.	Males.	Females.	Sex not stated.	Total.
Merchants	14759	....	...	14759
Farmers	34693	....	...	34693
Mechanics	14997	....	...	14997
Mariners	1156	....	...	1156
Miners	232	....	...	232
Laborers	42580	....	...	42580
Shoemakers	45	....	...	45
Tailors	28	....	...	28
Seamstresses and Milliners	....	201	...	201
Weavers and Spinners	92	89	...	181
Actors and Actresses	21	9	...	30
Physicians	247	....	...	247
Clergymen	149	....	...	149
Lawyers	224	....	...	224
Clerks	242	....	...	242
Masons	18	....	...	18
Manufacturers	60	....	...	60
Musicians	42	2	...	44
Engineers	144	....	...	144
Printers	34	....	...	34
Painters	16	....	...	16
Artists	53	1	...	54
Butchers	19	....	...	19
Teachers	26	6	...	32
Millers	67	....	...	67
Bakers	23	....	...	23
Servants	62	2536	...	2598
Other occupations	566	37	...	603
Not stated	29586	87402	12	117000
Total	140181	90283	12	230476

IV.—COUNTRY WHERE BORN.

COUNTRIES.	Males.	Females.	Sex not stated.	Total.
England	21986	16885	...	38871
Ireland	26029	23598	...	49627
Scotland	3173	2102	...	5275
Wales	635	541	...	1176
Great Britain and Ireland	1198	1052	...	2250
British America	5367	2394	...	7761
France	3869	2175	...	6044
Spain	748	200	3	951
Portugal	169	36	...	205
Switzerland	2488	1945	...	4433
Belgium	819	687	...	1506
Prussia	3187	2512	...	5699
Germany	37356	28863	...	66219
Holland	1482	1106	...	2588
Denmark	287	241	...	528
Norway and Sweden	448	373	...	821
Poland	300	162	...	462
Russia	12	1	...	13
Turkey	7	2	...	9
Italy	837	187	...	1024
Sardinia	5	....	...	5
Sicily	21	2	...	23
China	3524	2	...	3526
East Indies	3	3	...	6
Australia	2	2	...	4
Asia	7	1	...	8
Azores	138	37	...	175
Society Islands	....	1	...	1
Madeira	....	1	...	1
St. Helena	....	1	...	1
Africa	14	....	...	14
Sandwich Islands	4	3	...	7
South America	151	40	...	191
Central America	1	....	...	1
Mexico	309	111	...	420
West Indies	644	243	...	887
United States	24874	4716	9	29599
Not stated	87	58	...	145
Total	140181	90283	12	230476
Born in the United States	24874	4716	9	29599
Aliens	115307	85567	3	200877

COMPARATIVE STATEMENTS.

Statement of the TOTAL NUMBER of passengers arriving to the United States by sea from foreign countries, from September 30, 1819, to December 31, 1855.

YEAR.	Males.	Females.	Sex not stated.	Total.
Year ending Sept. 30, 1820 .	6,447	2,680	1,184	10,311
" " " " 1821 .	6,866	1,938	2,840	11,644
" " " " 1822 .	5,318	1,149	2,082	8,549
" " " " 1823 .	5,313	1,044	1,908	8,265
" " " " 1824 .	6,253	1,561	1,813	9,627
" " " " 1825 .	9,206	3,329	323	12,858
" " " " 1826 .	10,218	3,633	57	13,908
" " " " 1827 .	14,165	6,479	1,133	21,777
" " " " 1828 .	19,446	10,677	61	30,184
" " " " 1829 .	12,938	5,470	6,105	24,513
" " " " 1830 .	7,514	3,575	13,748	24,837
" " " " 1831 .	15,917	7,963	....	23,880
" " " " 1832 .	35,599	18,752	....	54,351
Quarter ending Dec. 31, 1832 .	4,691	2,512	100	7.303
Year ending Dec. 31, 1833 .	42,548	17,377	....	59,925
" " " " 1834 .	40,730	23,180	4,038	67,948
" " " " 1835 .	30,752	17,791	173	48,716
" " " " 1836 .	51,459	28,689	824	80,972
" " " " 1837 .	53,403	28,706	2,850	84,959
" " " " 1838 .	28,504	14,900	1,755	45,159
" " " " 1839 .	48,200	26,454	12	74,666
" " " " 1840 .	58,998	33,158	51	92,207
" " " " 1841 .	53,815	33,814	176	87,805
" " " " 1842 .	67,124	43,475	381	110,980
First three quarters of 1843 .	33,172	23,354	3	56,529
Year ending Sept. 30, 1844 .	48,897	35,867	....	84,764
" " " " 1845 .	69,179	49,311	1,406	119,896
" " " " 1846 .	90,974	66,778	897	158,649
" " " " 1847 .	139,167	99,325	990	239,482
" " " " 1848 .	136,128	92,883	472	229,483
" " " " 1849 .	179,256	119,915	512	299,683
" " " " 1850 .	200,904	113,392	1,038	315,334
Quarter ending Dec. 31, 1850 .	38,282	27,107	181	65,570
Year ending Dec. 31, 1851 .	245,017	163,745	66	408,828
" " " " 1852 .	235,731	160,174	1,438	397,343
" " " " 1853 .	236,732	164,178	72	400,982
" " " " 1854 .	284,887	175,587	....	460,474
" " " " 1855 .	140,181	90,283	12	230,476
Total	2,713,931	1,720,205	48,701	4,482,837

Statement of the NUMBER of ALIEN passengers arriving in the United States by sea from foreign countries, from September 30, 1819, to December 31, 1855.

YEAR.	Males.	Females.	Sex not stated.	Total.
Year ending Sept. 30, 1820 .	4,871	2,393	1,121	8,385
" " " " 1821 .	4,651	1,636	2,840	9,127
" " " " 1822 .	3,816	1,013	2,082	6,911
" " " " 1823 .	3,598	848	1,908	6,354
" " " " 1824 .	4,706	1,393	1,813	7,912
" " " " 1825 .	6,917	2,959	323	10,199
" " " " 1826 .	7,702	3,078	57	10,837
" " " " 1827 .	11,803	5,939	1,133	18,875
" " " " 1828 .	17,261	10,060	61	27,382
" " " " 1829 .	11,303	5,112	6,105	22,520
" " " " 1830 .	6,439	3,135	13,748	23,322
" " " " 1831 .	14,909	7,724	....	22,633
" " " " 1832 .	34,596	18,583	....	53,179
Quarter ending Dec. 31, 1832 .	4,691	2,512	100	7,303
Year ending Dec. 31, 1833 .	41,546	17,094	....	58,640
" " " " 1834 .	38,796	22,540	4,029	65,365
" " " " 1835 .	28,196	17,027	151	45,374
" " " " 1836 .	47,865	27,553	824	76,242
" " " " 1837 .	48,837	27,653	2,850	79,340
" " " " 1838 .	23,474	13,685	1,755	38,914
" " " " 1839 .	42,932	25,125	12	68,069
" " " " 1840 .	52,883	31,132	51	84,066
" " " " 1841 .	48,082	32,031	176	80,289
" " " " 1842 .	62,277	41,907	381	104,565
First three quarters of 1843 .	30,069	22,424	3	52,496
Year ending Sept. 30, 1844 .	44,431	34,184	....	78,615
" " " " 1845 .	65,015	48,115	1,241	114,371
" " " " 1846 .	87,777	65,742	897	154,416
" " " " 1847 .	136,086	97,917	965	234,968
" " " " 1848 .	133,906	92,149	472	226,527
" " " " 1849 .	177,232	119,280	512	297,024
" " " " 1850 .	196,331	112,635	1,038	310,004
Quarter ending Dec. 31, 1850 .	32,990	26,805	181	59,976
Year ending Dec. 31, 1851 .	217,181	162,219	66	379,466
" " " " 1852 .	212,469	157,696	1,438	371,603
" " " " 1853 .	207,958	160,615	72	368,645
" " " " 1854 .	256,177	171,656	....	427,833
" " " " 1855 .	115,307	85,567	3	200,877
Total. . . .	2,485,080	1,679,136	48,408	4,212,624

Statement of the number of passengers born in ENGLAND, IRELAND, SCOTLAND, WALES, and "GREAT BRITAIN AND IRELAND," arriving in the United States by sea from foreign countries, from September 30, 1819, to December 31, 1855.

YEAR ENDING	England.	Ireland.	Scotland.	Wales.	Great Britain and Ireland.	Total.
Sept. 30, 1820 .	1,782	1,725	268	....	2,249	6,024
" " 1821 .	1,036	1,518	293	11	1,870	4,728
" " 1822 .	856	1,346	198	13	1,075	3,488
" " 1823 .	851	1,051	180	69	857	3,008
" " 1824 .	713	1,575	257	33	1,031	3,609
" " 1825 .	1,002	4,157	113	11	1,700	6,983
" " 1826 .	1,459	3,333	230	6	2,699	7,727
" " 1827 .	2,521	3,282	460	....	7,689	13,952
" " 1828 .	2,735	5,266	1,041	17	8,781	17,840
" " 1829 .	2,149	3,106	111	3	5,225	10,594
" " 1830 .	733	.747	29	7	2,358	3,874
" " 1831 .	251	1,647	226	131	5,992	8,247
" " 1832 .	944	5,120	158	....	11,545	17,767
* Dec. 31, 1832 .	....	....	......	....	....	....
Dec. 31, 1833 .	2,966	4,511	1,921	29	4,137	13,564
" " 1834 .	1,129	6,772	110	1	26,952	34,964
" " 1835 .	468	5,148	63	16	24,202	29,897
" " 1836 .	420	2,152	106	2	41,004	43,684
" " 1837 .	896	737	14	6	39,073	40,726
" " 1838 .	157	1,225	48	....	16,635	18,065
" " 1839 .	62	1,199	......	....	32,973	34,234
" " 1840 .	318	677	21	....	41,027	42,043
" " 1841 .	147	3,291	35	55	50,432	53,960
" " 1842 .	1,743	4,844	24	38	66,698	73,347
First 3 qrs. of 1843	3,517	1,173	41	....	23,369	28,100
Sept. 30, 1844 .	1,357	5,491	23	3	40,969	47,843
" " 1845 .	1,710	8,641	368	11	53,301	64,031
" " 1846 .	2,854	12,949	305	147	57,677	73,932
" " 1847 .	3,476	29,640	337	145	95,240	128,838
" " 1848 .	4,455	24,802	659	348	117,829	148,093
" " 1849 .	6,036	31,321	1,060	272	175,841	214,530
" " 1850 .	5,276	27,674	627	49	141,859	175,485
* Dec. 31, 1850 .	1,521	12,506	233	193	25,151	39,604
Dec. 31, 1851 .	5,306	55,874	966	211	210,383	272,740
" " 1852 .	30,007	159,548	8,148	741	1,803	200,247
" " 1853 .	28,867	162,649	6,006	222	2,481	200,225
" " 1854 .	48,901	101,606	4,605	816	4,325	160,253
" " 1855 .	38,871	49,627	5,275	1,176	2,250	97,199
Total . .	207,492	747,930	34,559	4,782	1,348,682	2,343,445

* Quarter ending.

Statement of the number of passengers born in FRANCE, SPAIN, PORTUGAL, BELGIUM, PRUSSIA, and GERMANY, arriving in the United States by sea from foreign countries, from September 30, 1819, to December 31, 1855.

YEAR ENDING	France.	Spain.	Portu-gal.	Belgium.	Prussia.	Germany.
Sept. 30, 1820 .	371	139	35	1	20	948
" " 1821 .	370	191	18	2	18	365
" " 1822 .	351	152	28	10	9	139
" " 1823 .	460	220	24	2	4	179
" " 1824 .	377	359	13	1	6	224
" " 1825 .	515	273	13	1	2	448
" " 1826 .	545	436	16	2	16	495
" " 1827 .	1,280	414	7	7	7	425
" " 1828 .	2,843	209	14	2	45	1,806
" " 1829 .	582	202	9	......	15	582
" " 1830 .	1,174	21	3	......	4	1,972
" " 1831 .	2,038	37	......	1	18	2,395
" " 1832 .	5,361	106	5	......	26	10,168
* Dec. 31, 1832 .	....	......	......	......	....	....
Dec. 31, 1833 .	4,682	516	633	......	165	6,823
" " 1834 .	2,989	107	44	3	32	17,654
" " 1835 .	2,696	183	29	1	66	8,245
" " 1836 .	4,443	180	29	......	568	20,139
" " 1837 .	5,074	230	34	......	704	23,036
" " 1838 .	3,675	202	24	14	314	11,369
" " 1839 .	7,198	428	19	1	1,234	19,794
" " 1840 .	7,419	136	12	2	1,123	28,581
" " 1841 .	5,006	215	7	106	1,564	13,727
" " 1842 .	4,504	122	15	44	2,083	18,287
First 3 qrs. of 1843	3,346	145	32	135	3,009	11,432
Sept. 30, 1844 .	3,155	270	16	165	1,505	19,226
" " 1845 .	7,663	304	14	541	1,217	33,138
" " 1846 .	10,583	73	2	43	551	57,010
" " 1847 .	20,040	158	5	1,473	837	73,444
" " 1848 .	7,743	164	67	897	451	58,014
" " 1849 .	5,841	329	26	590	173	60,062
" " 1850 .	8,009	325	366	1,055	14	63,168
* Dec. 31, 1850 .	1,372	104	......	25	745	14,969
Dec. 31, 1851 .	20,126	435	50	......	1,160	71,322
" " 1852 .	6,763	391	68	8	2,343	143,575
" " 1853 .	10,770	1,091	95	87	1,293	140,653
" " 1854 .	13,317	1,433	72	266	8,955	206,054
" " 1855 .	6,044	951	205	1,506	5,699	66,219
Total . .	188,725	11,251	2,049	6,991	35,995	1,206,087

* Quarter ending.

Statement of the number of passengers born in HOLLAND, DENMARK, NORWAY AND SWEDEN, POLAND, RUSSIA, TURKEY, arriving in the United States by sea from foreign countries, from September 30, 1819, to December 31, 1855.

YEAR.	Holland.	Denmark.	Norway and Sweden.	Poland.	Russia.	Turkey.
Year ending Sept. 30, 1820 .	49	20	3	5	14	1
" " " " 1821 .	56	12	12	1	7	...
" " " " 1822 .	51	18	10	3	10	4
" " " " 1823 .	19	6	1	3	7	2
" " " " 1824 .	40	11	9	4	7	2
" " " " 1825 .	37	14	4	1	10	...
" " " " 1826 .	176	10	16	....	4	2
" " " " 1827 .	245	15	13	1	19	1
" " " " 1828 .	263	50	10	1	7	6
" " " " 1829 .	169	17	13	....	1	1
" " " " 1830 .	22	16	3	2	3	2
" " " " 1831 .	175	23	13	....	1	...
" " " " 1832 .	205	21	313	34	52	...
Quarter ending Dec. 31, 1832 .	......	....	......	....	...	...
Year ending Dec. 31, 1833 .	39	173	16	1	159	1
" " " " 1834 .	87	24	42	54	15	1
" " " " 1835 .	124	37	31	54	9	...
" " " " 1836 .	301	416	57	53	2	3
" " " " 1837 .	312	109	290	81	19	...
" " " " 1838 .	27	52	60	41	13	...
" " " " 1839 .	85	56	324	46	7	1
" " " " 1840 .	57	152	55	5	...	1
" " " " 1841 .	214	31	195	15	174	6
" " " " 1842 .	330	35	553	10	28	2
First three quarters of 1843 .	330	29	1,748	17	6	5
Year ending Sept. 30, 1844 .	184	25	1,311	36	13	10
" " " " 1845 .	791	54	928	6	1	3
" " " " 1846 .	979	114	1,916	4	248	4
" " " " 1847 .	2,631	13	1,307	8	5	2
" " " " 1848 .	918	210	903	....	1	3
" " " " 1849 .	1,190	8	3,473	4	44	9
" " " " 1850 .	576	10	1,363	3	31	13
Quarter ending Dec. 31, 1850 .	108	10	206	2	...	2
Year ending Dec. 31, 1851 .	352	14	2,424	10	1	2
" " " " 1852 .	1,719	3	4,103	110	2	3
" " " " 1853 .	600	32	3,364	33	3	15
" " " " 1854 .	1,534	691	3,531	208	2	7
" " " " 1855 .	2,588	528	821	462	13	9
Total	17,583	3,059	29,441	1,318	938	123

Statement of the number of passengers born in SWITZERLAND, ITALY, GREECE, SICILY, SARDINIA, CORSICA, MALTA, and "EUROPE," arriving in the United States by sea from foreign countries, from September 30, 1819, to December 31, 1855.

YEAR.	Switzerland.	Italy.	Greece.	Sicily.	Sardinia.	Corsica.	Malta.	Europe.
Year ending Sept. 30, 1820 .	31	25	...	...	5	..	...	2
" " " " 1821 .	93	62	...	...	...	..	...	...
" " " " 1822 .	110	32	...	2	1	..	...	...
" " " " 1823 .	47	32	...	...	1	1	...	...
" " " " 1824 .	253	41	5	2	2	..	...	...
" " " " 1825 .	166	58	...	...	17	..	1	...
" " " " 1826 .	245	50	4	1	6	..	...	...
" " " " 1827 .	297	35	...	...	...	1	...	...
" " " " 1828 .	1,592	30	7	4	...	..	...	...
" " " " 1829 .	314	16	1	7	...	..	...	...
" " " " 1830 .	109	8	3	1	...	..	...	...
" " " " 1831 .	63	28	...	...	...	..	...	...
" " " " 1832 .	129	2	1	1	...	2	...	...
Quarter ending Dec. 31, 1832 .	......	....	...	...	...	..	...	...
Year ending Dec. 31, 1833 .	634	1,693	1	6	...	..	5	...
" " " " 1834 .	1,389	103	...	1	1	..	...	...
" " " " 1835 .	548	56	7	4	...	..	...	...
" " " " 1836 .	445	107	28	8	...	..	2	...
" " " " 1837 .	383	36	5	...	...	..	...	...
" " " " 1838 .	123	82	4	4	...	1	...	...
" " " " 1839 .	607	76	...	2	6	2	28	...
" " " " 1840 .	500	28	3	9	...	..	...	...
" " " " 1841 .	751	166	...	13	...	..	66	...
" " " " 1842 .	483	93	1	4	3	1	1	...
First three quarters of 1843 .	553	108	4	3	6	..	5	...
Year ending Sept. 30, 1844 .	839	79	3	4	58	1	2	48
" " " " 1845 .	471	63	2	5	69	..	...	...
" " " " 1846 .	698	88	3	4	59	..	4	...
" " " " 1847 .	192	160	...	4	...	..	...	...
" " " " 1848 .	319	219	1	22	...	..	...	...
" " " " 1849 .	13	208	...	1	...	..	...	...
" " " " 1850 .	146	360	2	10	3	..	...	...
Quarter ending Dec. 31, 1850 .	179	46	...	9	3	..	...	3
Year ending Dec. 31, 1851 .	427	423	...	24	...	..	...	...
" " " " 1852 .	2,788	297	10	44	10	..	...	473
" " " " 1853 .	2,748	267	12	56	232	..	...	...
" " " " 1854 .	7,953	984	1	60	219	..	2	...
" " " " 1855 .	4,433	1,024	...	23	5	..	...	...
Total	31,071	7,185	108	338	706	9	116	526

Statement of the number of passengers born in BRITISH AMERICA, SOUTH AMERICA, CENTRAL AMERICA, MEXICO, and the WEST INDIES, arriving in the United States by sea from foreign countries, from September 30, 1819, to December 31, 1855.

YEAR.	British America.	South America.	Central America.	Mexico.	West Indies.
Year ending Sept. 30, 1820 .	209	11	2	1	164
" " " " 1821 .	184	8	....	4	107
" " " " 1822 .	204	7	3	5	159
" " " " 1823 .	167	20	....	35	160
" " " " 1824 .	155	25	10	110	259
" " " " 1825 .	314	67	8	68	389
" " " " 1826 .	223	63	12	106	427
" " " " 1827 .	165	54	7	127	227
" " " " 1828 .	267	77	5	1,089	652
" " " " 1829 .	409	73	10	2,290	517
" " " " 1830 .	189	137	50	983	937
" " " " 1831 .	176	42	3	692	1,281
" " " " 1832 .	608	174	6	827	1,256
Quarter ending Dec. 31, 1832 .	......	......	....	......	....
Year ending Dec. 31, 1833 .	1,194	27	18	779	1,264
" " " " 1834 .	1,020	74	9	885	791
" " " " 1835 .	1,193	145	4	1,032	938
" " " " 1836 .	2,814	146	....	798	1,178
" " " " 1837 .	1,279	91	4	627	1,627
" " " " 1838 .	1,476	72	....	211	1,231
" " " " 1839 .	1,926	49	....	353	1,289
" " " " 1840 .	1,938	36	....	395	1,446
" " " " 1841 .	1,816	219	....	352	1,042
" " " " 1842 .	2,078	102	1	403	1,410
First three quarters of 1843 .	1,502	62	12	398	880
Year ending Sept. 30, 1844 .	2,711	61	....	197	771
" " " " 1845 .	3,195	80	21	498	1,241
" " " " 1846 .	3,855	92	5	222	1,351
" " " " 1847 .	3,827	70	21	62	1,251
" " " " 1848 .	6,473	150	4	24	1,338
" " " " 1849 .	6,890	190	233	518	1,073
" " " " 1850 .	7,796	2,462	71	498	2,903
Quarter ending Dec. 31, 1850 .	1,580	91	....	99	268
Year ending Dec. 31, 1851 .	7,438	59	96	181	1,929
" " " " 1852 .	6,352	39	....	72	1,232
" " " " 1853 .	5,424	38	....	162	406
" " " " 1854 .	6,891	136	24	446	1,036
" " " " 1855 .	7,761	191	1	420	887
Total	91,699	5,440	640	15,969	35,317

Statement of the number of passengers born in CHINA, the EAST INDIES, PERSIA, and "ASIA," arriving in the United States by sea from foreign countries, from September 30, 1819, to December 31, 1855.

YEAR.	China.	East Indies.	Persia.	Asia.	Total.
Year ending Sept. 30, 1820 .	1	1	....	3	5
" " " " 1821 .	......	....	....	......	....
" " " " 1822 .	......	1	....	......	1
" " " " 1823 .	......	....	....	......	....
" " " " 1824 .	......	1	....	......	1
" " " " 1825 .	1	....	....	......	1
" " " " 1826 .	......	1	....	......	1
" " " " 1827 .	......	1	....	......	1
" " " " 1828 .	......	3	....	......	3
" " " " 1829 .	1	1	....	......	2
" " " " 1830 .	......	....	....	......	....
" " " " 1831 .	......	1	....	......	1
" " " " 1832 .	......	4	....	......	4
Quarter ending Dec. 31, 1832 .	......	....	....	......	....
Year ending Dec. 31, 1833 .	......	3	....	......	3
" " " " 1834 .	......	6	....	......	6
" " " " 1835 .	8	8	....	1	17
" " " " 1836 .	......	4	....	......	4
" " " " 1837 .	......	11	....	......	11
" " " " 1838 .	......	1	....	......	1
" " " " 1839 .	......	....	....	......	....
" " " " 1840 .	......	1	....	......	1
" " " " 1841 .	2	1	....	......	3
" " " " 1842 .	4	2	1	......	7
First three quarters of 1843 .	3	2	6	......	11
Year ending Sept. 30, 1844 .	3	1	....	2	6
" " " " 1845 .	6	....	....	......	6
" " " " 1846 .	7	4	....	......	11
" " " " 1847 .	4	8	....	......	12
" " " " 1848 .	......	6	....	2	8
" " " " 1849 .	3	8	....	......	11
" " " " 1850 .	3	4	....	......	7
Quarter ending Dec. 31, 1850 .	......	....	....	......	....
Year ending Dec. 31, 1851 .	......	2	....	......	2
" " " " 1852 .	......	4	....	......	4
" " " " 1853 .	42	5	....	......	47
" " " " 1854 .	13,100	....	....	......	13,100
" " " " 1855 .	3,526	6	....	8	3,540
Total. . . .	16,714	101	7	16	16,838

Statement of the number of passengers born in LIBERIA, EGYPT, MOROCCO, ALGIERS, the "BARBARY STATES," CAPE OF GOOD HOPE, and "AFRICA," arriving in the United States by sea from foreign countries, from September 30, 1819, to December 31, 1855.*

YEAR.	Liberia.	Egypt.	Morocco.	Algiers.	Barbary States.	Cape of Good Hope.	Africa.	Total.
Year ending Sept. 30, 1820 .	....	...	...	..	....	....	1	1
" " " " 1821 .	....	...	...	..	....	2	....	2
" " " " 1825 .	....	...	...	..	1	....	....	1
" " " " 1827 .	....	...	...	..	3	....	1	4
" " " " 1828 .	....	...	...	..	....	....	6	6
" " " " 1829 .	1	...	...	..	....	....	....	1
" " " " 1830 .	....	...	...	..	....	....	2	2
" " " " 1831 .	....	...	...	..	....	....	2	2
" " " " 1832 .	....	...	...	..	....	....	2	2
" " Dec. 31, 1833 .	....	...	...	..	....	....	1	1
" " " " 1834 .	....	...	...	..	....	....	1	1
" " " " 1835 .	....	...	...	..	....	....	14	14
" " " " 1836 .	....	...	...	..	....	....	6	6
" " " " 1837 .	....	...	...	..	....	....	2	2
" " " " 1838 .	....	4	4	..	....	....	2	10
" " " " 1839 .	8	...	...	..	....	....	....	8
" " " " 1840 .	....	...	...	..	....	....	6	6
" " " " 1841 .	....	...	...	..	....	....	14	14
" " " " 1842 .	....	...	...	..	....	....	3	3
First three quarters of 1843 .	....	...	...	..	....	....	6	6
Year ending Sept. 30, 1844 .	5	...	...	..	....	....	9	14
" " " " 1845 .	....	...	...	1	....	....	3	4
" " " " 1846 .	....	...	...	1	....	....	....	1
" " " " 1848 .	....	...	...	..	....	....	10	10
" " " " 1849 .	....	...	1	..	....	....	2	3
" " Dec. 31, 1851 .	....	...	...	..	....	....	3	3
" " " " 1853 .	....	...	...	..	....	....	8	8
" " " " 1855 .	....	...	...	..	....	....	14	14
Total	14	4	5	2	4	2	118	149

* During the periods omitted, there were no arrivals of passengers born in any part of Africa.

Statement of the number of passengers born in the AZORES, CANARY, MADEIRA, CAPE VERDE, SANDWICH, and SOCIETY ISLANDS, arriving in the United States by sea from foreign countries, from September 30, 1819, to December 31, 1855.

YEAR.	Azores.	Canary Islands.	Madeira Islands.	Cape Verde Islands.	Sandwich Islands.	Society Islands.
Year ending Sept. 30, 1820 .	3	3	....	....	1	....
" " " " 1821 .	......	......	1	....	....	....
" " " " 1822 .	......	......	5	1	....	....
" " " " 1823 .	......	1	.....	1	....	....
" " " " 1824 .	......	1	.....	....	....	....
" " " " 1825 .	1	6	1	1	....	....
" " " " 1826 .	......	12	.....	1	....	....
" " " " 1827 .	4	......	1	....	....	....
" " " " 1828 .	3	5	9	....	....	....
" " " " 1829 .	1	243	46	....	....	....
" " " " 1830 .	1	......	7	....	....	....
" " " " 1831 .	......	......	1	1	1	....
" " " " 1832 .	5	......	.....	....	....	....
Quarter ending Dec. 31, 1832 .	......	......	.....	....	....	....
Year ending Dec. 31, 1833 .	3	3	2	....	....	....
" " " " 1834 .	1	3	25	3	....	....
" " " " 1835 .	2	......	4	11	3	....
" " " " 1836 .	......	......	5	....	2	....
" " " " 1837 .	......	......	5	....	....	....
" " " " 1838 .	6	......	2	....	....	....
" " " " 1839 .	7	......	.....	....	....	....
" " " " 1840 .	5	......	8	....	....	....
" " " " 1841 .	3	......	.....	....	3	....
" " " " 1842 .	4	1	.....	....	....	....
First three quarters of 1843 .	8	......	.....	....	4	1
Year ending Sept. 30, 1844 .	23	......	.....	1	....	....
" " " " 1845 .	5	......	.....	2	....	....
" " " " 1846 .	15	......	.....	....	....	....
" " " " 1847 .	21	......	3	....	1	....
" " " " 1848 .	20	......	.....	....	3	....
" " " " 1849 .	48	......	.....	....	....	....
" " " " 1850 .	180	......	.....	....	17	....
Quarter ending Dec. 31, 1850 .	......	......	.....	....	....	....
Year ending Dec. 31, 1851 .	103	......	8	....	....	....
" " " " 1852 .	178	......	.....	....	....	....
" " " " 1853 .	209	......	55	....	....	....
" " " " 1854 .	254	......	14	....	17	3
" " " " 1855 .	175	......	1	....	7	1
Total. . . .	1,288	278	203	22	59	5

Statement of the number of passengers born in AUSTRALIA, ST. HELENA, the ISLE OF FRANCE, and SOUTH SEA ISLANDS, arriving in the United States by sea from foreign countries from September 30, 1819, to December 31, 1855.*

YEAR.	Australia.	St. Helena.	Isle of France.	South Sea Islands.
Year ending September 30, 1822	2	....	....	......
" " " " 1827	....	....	....	79
" " December 31, 1835	....	1	....	......
" " " " 1838	....	....	2	......
" " " " 1839	1	....	....	......
" " " " 1840	2	....	....	......
" " September 30, 1846	....	3	....	......
" " " " 1849	....	....	1	......
" " December 31, 1851	....	2	....	......
" " " " 1852	....	4	....	......
" " " " 1854	11	3	....	......
" " " " 1855	4	1	....	......
Total	20	14	3	79

* During the periods omitted, there were no arrivals of passengers born in the Islands mentioned in this Statement.

RECAPITULATION.

COUNTRIES.	Total arrivals.	COUNTRIES.	Total arrivals.
England	207,492	West Indies . . .	35,317
Ireland	747,930	China	16,714
Scotland	34,559	East Indies . . .	101
Wales	4,782	Persia	7
Great Britain and Ireland	1,348,682	Asia	16
France.	188,725	Liberia	14
Spain	11,251	Egypt	4
Portugal	2,049	Morocco.	5
Belgium	6,991	Algiers	2
Prussia	35,995	Barbary States .	4
Germany	1,206,087	Cape of Good Hope	2
Holland	17,583	Africa	118
Denmark	3,059	Azores	1,288
Norway and Sweden	29,441	Canary Islands .	278
Poland	1,318	Madeira Islands .	203
Russia	938	Cape Verde Islands	22
Turkey	123	Sandwich Islands	59
Switzerland . . .	31,071	Society Islands .	5
Italy	7,185	Australia	20
Greece	108	St. Helena . . .	14
Sicily	338	Isle of France . .	3
Sardinia	706	South Sea Islands	79
Corsica	9	Not stated. . . .	157,537
Malta	116	United States . .	270,213
Europe	526		
British America .	91,699		
South America .	5,440		
Central America	640		
Mexico	15,969	Total arrivals during the $36\frac{1}{4}$ y'rs ending December 31, 1855 . .	4,482,837

APPENDIX,

CONTAINING

NATURALIZATION AND PASSENGER LAWS

OF THE UNITED STATES, AND EXTRACTS FROM THE LAWS OF THE SEVERAL STATES RELATIVE TO IMMIGRANTS, THE IMPORTATION OF PAUPERS, CONVICTS, LUNATICS, ETC.

LAWS OF THE UNITED STATES

RELATIVE TO

NATURALIZATION.

REMARKS.

An Act of Congress to establish a uniform rule of naturalization, and to repeal all former laws passed on that subject, was approved April 14, 1802.

This Act contained certain provisions in favor of aliens residing in the United States at any time previous to the 29th of January, 1795 [see page 191], and certain other provisions in favor of those who resided in the United States at any time between the 29th of January, 1795, and the 18th of June, 1799 [see page 192].

By this Act, any alien arriving in the United States after the latter period was required, besides other conditions, to comply with the following before he could be admitted to the rights of citizenship:—

1. He shall declare on oath or affirmation, in some competent court, at least three years before his admission, that it was, *bona fide*, his intention to renounce for ever all allegiance to any sovereign or state of which he was a subject. [See page 190.]

2. He shall swear or affirm that he will support the Constitution of the United States. [See page 190.]

3. He shall satisfy the court that he has resided within the United States at least five years, and within the State or Territory where such court is held at least one year, before he can be admitted. It must further appear to the satisfaction of the court that he has behaved as a man of good moral character, attached to the principles of the Constitution, and well disposed to the good order and happiness of the United States. [See page 190.]

4. He shall renounce every title of nobility held by him. [See page 190.]

Subsequent laws modified this act in the following important particulars:—

A residence in the United States for the continued term of five years, without being at any time without the territory of the same, was required of aliens by an act approved March 3, 1813. [See page 195.] This provision, however, was repealed by the act of June 26, 1848. [See page 198.]

An Act approved May 26, 1824, provided that, instead of three years, as required by the Act of April 14, 1802, a declaration made two years before admission, shall be deemed sufficient. [See page 197.]

Such of the laws of the United States, relative to naturalization, as contain provisions at present in force, are herewith published.

April 14, 1802.

AN ACT to establish a uniform rule of naturalization, and to repeal the acts heretofore passed on that subject.

An alien may become a citizen of the United States.

Be it enacted by the Senate and House of Representatives of the United States of America, in Congress assembled, That any alien, being a free white person, may be admitted to become a citizen of the United States, or any of them, on the following conditions and not otherwise:—

On what conditions:

To declare, on oath or affirmation, in the supreme or superior court, or district or circuit court, of some one of the States or of the United States, three years before his admission, his intention to renounce forever his allegiance to any sovereign or state to which he is a subject.

First. That he shall have declared, on oath or affirmation, before the supreme, superior, district, or circuit court of some one of the States or of the territorial districts of the United States, or a circuit or district court of the United States, three years at least before his admission, that it was, *bona fide*, his intention to become a citizen of the United States, and to renounce for ever all allegiance and fidelity to any foreign prince, potentate, state, or sovereignty whatever, and particularly, by name, the prince, potentate, state, or sovereignty whereof such alien may, at the time, be a citizen or subject.

To swear or affirm that he will support the constitution of the United States.

Secondly. That he shall, at the time of his application to be admitted, declare on oath or affirmation, before some one of the courts aforesaid, that he will support the constitution of the United States, and that he doth absolutely and entirely renounce and abjure all allegiance and fidelity to every foreign prince, potentate, state, or sovereignty whatever, and particularly, by name, the prince, potentate, state, or sovereignty whereof he was before a citizen or subject; which proceedings shall be recorded by the clerk of the court.

That he shall have resided in the U. States five years before he shall be admitted a citizen.

Shall prove that he is a man of good moral character and attached to the constitution of the U. States.

Thirdly. That the court admitting such alien shall be satisfied that he has resided within the United States five years at least, and within the State or Territory where such court is at the time held one year at least; and it shall further appear to their satisfaction, that during that time he has behaved as a man of a good moral character, attached to the principles of the constitution of the United States, and well-disposed to the good order and happiness of the same: *Provided,* That the oath of the applicant shall, in no case, be allowed to prove his residence.

Fourthly. That in case the alien applying to be admitted to citizenship shall have borne any hereditary title, or been of any of the orders of nobility in the kingdom or state from which he came, he shall, in addition to the above requisites, make an express renunciation of his title or order of nobility in the court to which his application shall be made; which renunciation shall be recorded in the said court: *Provided,* That no alien who shall be a native citizen, denizen, or subject of any country, state, or sovereign, with whom the United States shall be at war at the time of his application, shall be then admitted to be a citizen of the United States: *Provided, also,* That any alien who was residing within the limits and under the jurisdiction of the United States before the twenty-ninth day of January, one thousand seven hundred and ninety-five, may be admitted to become a citizen, on due proof, made to some one of the courts aforesaid, that he has resided two years, at least, within and under the jurisdiction of the United States, and one year, at least, immediately preceding his application, within the State or Territory where such court is at the time held; and on his declaring, on oath or affirmation, that he will support the constitution of the United States, and that he doth absolutely and entirely renounce and abjure all allegiance and fidelity to any foreign prince, potentate, state, or sovereignty whatever, and particularly, by name, the prince, potentate, state, or sovereignty whereof he was before a citizen or subject; and, moreover on its appearing, to the satisfaction of the court, that during the said term of two years he has behaved as a man of good moral character, attached to the constitution of the United States, and well disposed to the good order and happiness of the same; and where the alien applying for admission to citizenship shall have borne any hereditary title, or been of any of the orders of nobility in the kingdom or state from which he came, on his moreover making in the court an express renunciation of his title or order of nobility, before he shall be entitled to such admission; all of which proceedings, required in this proviso to be performed in the court, shall be recorded by the clerk thereof: *And provided, also,* That any alien who was residing within the limits and under the jurisdiction of the United States at any time between the said twenty-ninth day of January, one thousand seven hundred and ninety-five, and the eighteenth day of June, one thousand seven hundred and ninety-eight, may, within two years after the passing of this act, be admitted to become a citizen without a compliance with the first condition above specified.

Shall renounce every title of nobility held by him.

On what conditions an alien may be naturalized who resided in the United States before the 29th of January, 1795.

Proceedings to be recorded by the clerk of the court.

Provision in favor of persons residing in the U. States between the 29th of January, 1795, and the 18th of June, 1798.

Mode of naturalization prescribed.

SEC. 2. *Provided, also, and be it further enacted,* That, in addition to the directions aforesaid, all free white persons, being aliens, who may arrive in the United States after the passing of this act, shall, in order to become citizens of the United States, make registry and obtain certificates in the following manner to wit: every person desirous of being naturalized shall, if of the age of twenty-one years, make report of himself, or, if under the age of twenty-one years, or held in service, shall be reported by his parent, guardian, master, or mistress, to the clerk of the district court of the district where such alien or aliens shall arrive, or to some other court of record of the United States, of either of the territorial districts of the same, or of a particular State; and such report shall ascertain the name, birthplace, age, nation, and allegiance of each alien, together with the country whence he or she migrated, and the place of his or her intended settlement: and it shall be the duty of such clerk, on receiving such report, to record the same in his office, and to grant to the person making such report, and to each individual concerned therein, whenever he shall be required, a certificate, under his hand and seal of office, of such report and registry; and for receiving and registering each report of an individual or family, he shall receive fifty cents, and for each certificate granted pursuant to this act to an individual or family, fifty cents; and such certificate shall be exhibited to the court by every alien who may arrive in the United States after the passing of this act, on his application to be naturalized, as evidence of the time of his arrival within the United States.

Free white persons arriving in the U. States to be registered.

Form of register.

SEC. 3. *And whereas,* doubts have arisen whether certain courts of record in some of the States are included within the description of district or circuit courts: *Be it further enacted,* That every court of record in any individual State having common law jurisdiction, and a seal and clerk or prothonotary, shall be considered as a district court within the meaning of this act; and every alien who may have been naturalized in any such court, shall enjoy, from and after the passing of the act, the same rights and privileges as if he had been naturalized in a district or circuit court of the United States.

What courts are to be considered as capable of naturalizing aliens.

Children of persons naturalized under certain laws to be citizens of the United States.

SEC. 4. *And be it further enacted,* That the children of persons duly naturalized under any of the laws of the United States, or who, previous to the passing of any law on that subject by the government of the United States, may have become citizens of any one of the said States, under the laws thereof, being under the age of twenty-one years at the time of their parents being so naturalized or admitted to the rights of citizenship, shall, if dwelling in the United States, be considered as citizens of the United States; and the children of persons who now are or have been citizens of the United States shall, though born out of the limits and jurisdiction of the United States, be considered as citizens of the United States: *Provided*, That the right of citizenship shall not descend to persons whose fathers have never resided within the United States: *Provided, also*, That no person heretofore proscribed by any State, or who has been legally convicted of having joined the army of Great Britain during the late war, shall be admitted a citizen as aforesaid without the consent of the legislature of the State in which such person was proscribed.

Privilege of citizenship not to extend to children of persons who have never resided in the U. States; or to persons proscribed, &c.

SEC. 5. *And be it further enacted*, That all acts heretofore passed respecting naturalization be, and the same are hereby, repealed.

Repeal of former acts.

Approved, April 14, 1802.

AN ACT in addition to an act intitled "An act to establish a uniform rule of naturalization, and to repeal the acts heretofore passed on that subject."

March 26, 1804.

Be it enacted by the Senate and House of Representatives of the United States of America, in Congress assembled, That any alien, being a free white person, who was residing within the limits and under the jurisdiction of the United States at any time between the eighteenth day of June, one thousand seven hundred and ninety-eight, and the fourteenth day of April, one thousand eight hundred and two, and who has continued to reside within the same, may be admitted to become a citizen of the United States without a compliance with the first conditions specified in the first section of the act intituled "An act to establish a uniform rule of naturalization, and to repeal the acts heretofore passed on that subject."

Certain aliens permitted to become citizens of the U. States who resided in the U. States between the 18th June, 1798, and the 14th April, 1802.

Act of April 14, 1802.

SEC. 2. *And be it further enacted*, That when any alien who shall have complied with the first conditions specified in the first section of the said original act, and who shall have pursued the directions prescribed in the second section of said act, may die before he is actually naturalized, the widow and the children of such alien shall be considered as citizens of the United States, and shall be entitled to all rights and privileges as such, upon taking the oaths prescribed by law.

After an alien shall have complied with certain directions, his widow and children made citizens of the United States.

Approved, March 26, 1804.

March 3, 1813. AN ACT for the regulation of seamen on board the public and private vessels of the United States.

SEC. 12. *And be it further enacted,* That no person who shall arrive in the United States from and after the time when this act shall take effect, shall be admitted to become a citizen of the United States who shall not for the continued term of five years next preceding his admission as aforesaid have resided within the United States, without being at any time during the said five years out of the territory of the United States.

Residence of five years in the U. States necessary to qualify a person to become a citizen.

Approved, March 3, 1813.

July 30, 1813. AN ACT supplementary to the acts heretofore passed on the subject of a uniform rule of naturalization.

Be it enacted by the Senate and House of Representatives of the United States of America in Congress assembled, That persons resident within the United States, or the Territories thereof, on the eighteenth day of June, in the year one thousand eight hundred and twelve, who had before that day made a declaration, according to law, of their intentions to become citizens of the United States, or who, by the existing laws of the United States, were on that day entitled to become citizens without making such declaration, may be admitted to become citizens thereof, notwithstanding they shall be alien enemies at the times and in the manner prescribed by the laws heretofore passed on that subject: *Provided,* That nothing herein contained shall be taken or construed to interfere with or prevent the apprehension and removal, agreeably to law, of any alien enemy at any time previous to the actual naturalization of such alien.

Persons authorized to become citizens who were resident in the United States on the 18th June, 1812, and who had made a declaration of their intention to become citizens of the United States.

Proviso.

Approved, July 30, 1813.

March 22, 1816. AN ACT relative to evidence in cases of naturalization.

Be it enacted by the Senate and House of Representatives of the United States of America in Congress assembled, That the certificate of report and registry required as evidence of the time of arrival in the United States, according to the second section of the act of the fourteenth of April, one thousand eight hundred and two, entitled, "An act to establish a uniform rule of naturalization, and to repeal the acts heretofore passed on that subject," and also a certificate from the proper clerk or prothonotary of the declaration of intention, made before a

Evidence to be exhibited by aliens to become citizens of the United States.

Act of April 14, 1802.

court of record, and required as the first condition, according to the first section of said act, shall be exhibited by every alien, on his application to be admitted a citizen of the United States in pursuance of said act, who shall have arrived within the limits and under the jurisdiction of the United States since the eighteenth day of June, one thousand eight hundred and twelve, and shall each be recited at full length in the record of the court admitting such alien: otherwise he shall not be deemed to have complied with the conditions requisite for becoming a citizen of the United States; and any pretended admission of an alien who shall have arrived within the limits and under the jurisdiction of the United States since the said eighteenth day of June, one thousand eight hundred and twelve, to be a citizen, after the promulgation of this act, without such recital of each certificate at full length, shall be of no validity or effect under the act aforesaid.

Admissions without a recital of the proceeding, of no validity.

SEC. 2. *Provided, and be it enacted,* That nothing herein contained shall be construed to exclude from admission to citizenship any free white person who was residing within the limits and under the jurisdiction of the United States at any time between the eighteenth day of June, one thousand seven hundred and ninety-eight, and the fourteenth day of April, one thousand eight hundred and two, and who, having continued to reside therein without having made any declaration of intention before a court of record, as aforesaid, may be entitled to become a citizen of the United States according to the act of the 26th of March, one thousand eight hundred and four, entitled, "An act in addition to an act entitled, 'An act to establish a uniform rule of naturalization, and to repeal the acts heretofore passed on that subject.'" Whenever any person without a certificate of such declaration of intention as aforesaid shall make application to be admitted a citizen of the United States, it shall be proved, to the satisfaction of the court, that the applicant was residing within the limits and under the jurisdiction of the United States before the fourteenth day of April, one thousand eight hundred and two, and has continued to reside within the same, or he shall not be so admitted. And the residence of the applicant within the limits and under the jurisdiction of the United States for at least five years immediately preceding the time of such application shall be proved by the oath or affirmation of citizens of the United States; which citizens shall be named in the record as witnesses. And such continued residence within the limits and under the jurisdiction

Rights of persons heretofore settled in the U. States between the 18th June, 1798, and the 14th April, 1802.

Act of March 26, 1804.

Residence of the applicant to be naturalized.

Certificate of naturalization.

of the United States, when satisfactorily proved, and the place or places where the applicant has resided for at least five years, as aforesaid, shall be stated and set forth, together with the names of such citizens, in the record of the court admitting the applicant: otherwise the same shall not entitle him to be considered and deemed a citizen of the United States.

Approved, March 22, 1816.

May 26, 1824.

AN ACT in further addition to "An act to establish a uniform rule of naturalization, and to repeal the acts heretofore passed on that subject."

Be it enacted by the Senate and House of Representatives of the United States of America, in Congress assembled, That any alien, being a free white person, and a minor, under the age of twenty-one years, who shall have resided in the United States three years next preceding his arriving at the age of twenty-one years, and who shall have continued to reside therein to the time he may make application to be admitted a citizen thereof, may, after he arrives at the age of twenty-one years, and after he shall have resided five years within the United States, including the three years of his minority, be admitted a citizen of the United States without having made the declaration required in the first condition of the first section of the act to which this is an addition three years previous to his admission: *Provided,* Such alien shall make the declaration required therein at the time of his or her admission; and shall further declare, on oath, and prove, to the satisfaction of the court, that for three years next preceding it has been the *bona-fide* intention of such alien to become a citizen of the United States, and shall in all other respects comply with the laws in regard to naturalization.

Conditions on which an alien, being a free white person and a minor, may become a citizen of the United States.

Proviso.

SEC. 2. *And be it further enacted,* That no certificates of citizenship or naturalization heretofore obtained from any court of record within the United States shall be deemed invalid in consequence of an omission to comply with the requisition of the first section of the act entitled, "An act relative to evidence in cases of naturalization," passed the twenty-second day of March, one thousand eight hundred and sixteen.

No certificate of citizenship or naturalization, heretofore obtained from any court, to be deemed invalid.

Act of 1816.

SEC. 3. *And be it further enacted,* That the declaration required by the first condition specified in the first section of the act to which this is an addition shall, if the same has been *bona fide* made before the clerk of either of the courts in the said condition named, be as valid as if it had been made before the said courts respectively.

Declaration required by the first section of the former act to be valid on certain conditions.

SEC. 4. *And be it further enacted*, That a declaration by any alien, being a free white person, of his intended application to be admitted a citizen of the United States, made, in the manner and form prescribed in the first condition specified in the first section of the act to which this is in addition, two years before his admission, shall be a sufficient compliance with said condition, anything in the said act, or in any subsequent act, to the contrary notwithstanding.

A declaration of intention made two years before his admission shall be sufficient.

Approved, May 26, 1824.

AN ACT to amend the acts concerning naturalization.

May 24, 1828.

Be it enacted by the Senate and House of Representatives of the United States of America in Congress assembled, That the second section of the act entitled, "An act to establish a uniform rule of naturalization, and to repeal the acts heretofore passed on that subject," which was passed on the fourteenth day of April, one thousand eight hundred and two, and the first section of the act entitled, "An act relative to evidence in cases of naturalization," passed on the twenty-second day of March, one thousand eight hundred and sixteen, be, and the same are hereby, repealed.

Second section of the act of 14th April, 1802, and 22d March, 1816, repealed.

SEC. 2. *And be it further enacted*, That any alien, being a free white person, who was residing within the limits and under the jurisdiction of the United States between the fourteenth day of April, one thousand eight hundred and two, and the eighteenth day of June, one thousand eight hundred and twelve, and who has continued to reside within the same, may be admitted to become a citizen of the United States without having made any previous declaration of his intention to become a citizen: *Provided*, That whenever any person without a certificate of such declaration of intention shall make application to be admitted a citizen of the United States, it shall be proved, to the satisfaction of the court, that the applicant was residing within the limits and under the jurisdiction of the United States before the eighteenth day of June, one thousand eight hundred and twelve, and has continued to reside within the same, or he shall not be so admitted; and the residence of the applicant within the limits and under the jurisdiction of the United States for at least five years immediately preceding the time of such application shall be proved by the oath or affirmation of citizens of the United States, which citizens shall be named in the record as witnesses; and such

Any alien, being a free white person, who was residing within the limits, &c., of the United States between April 14, 1802, and June 18, 1812, to become a citizen.

Proviso.

continued residence within the limits and under the jurisdiction of the United States, when satisfactorily proved, and the place or places where the applicant has resided for at least five years, as aforesaid, shall be stated and set forth, together with the names of such citizens, in the record of the court admitting the applicant: otherwise the same shall not entitle him to be considered and deemed a citizen of the United States.

Approved, May 24, 1828.

June 26, 1848.

AN ACT to amend the act entitled, "An act for the regulation of seamen on board the public and private vessels of the United States," passed the third of March, eighteen hundred and thirteen.

Be it enacted by the Senate and House of Representatives of the United States of America in Congress assembled, That the last clause of the twelfth section of the act hereby amended, consisting of the following words, to wit, "without being at any time during the said five years out of the territory of the United States," be, and the same is hereby, repealed.

Repeal of clause of act of March 3, 1813, requiring a continued residence of five years in the United States previous to naturalization.

Approved, June 26, 1848.

LAWS OF THE SEVERAL STATES

RELATIVE TO

IMMIGRANTS, IMPORTATION OF PAUPERS, CONVICTS, LUNATICS, &c.

ALABAMA.

Captain of vessel bringing paupers to the State, to give bond to indemnify the State—Penalty for refusal.

Any person commanding any vessel which brings into this State any infant, lunatic, maimed, deaf, dumb, aged, or infirm person, who is likely to become chargeable to any county, may be brought before any judge of probate; and if such judge is satisfied that such person will probably be a charge to any county, he must require such master to enter into bond, payable to the State, with sureties resident in the State, to be approved by such judge, in the sum of five hundred dollars for each of such persons so brought, conditioned to pay all such expenses as any county in the State may incur in the support of such person; which bond must be filed and kept by such Judge; and on its condition being broken, may be sued on, and a recovery had in different actions to the amount of the penalty thereof, in the name of the State, for the use of any county; and on failure to give such bond, the judge must commit such master to jail until he gives the same, or is otherwise discharged by law. [Sec. 1219.] *Code of Alabama*, chap. 15, p. 268, 269.

CONNECTICUT.

Importing foreign convicts.

Sec. 115. No person convicted of any crime in a foreign country, and sentenced therefor to be transported abroad, shall be imported into this State; and every person who shall import or bring into this State any such convict, or aid or assist therein, knowing such person, so imported, to be a convict, and sentenced as aforesaid, shall be punished by a fine of three hundred and thirty-four dollars, for every such convict so imported. [*Revised Statutes*—1849, chap. 8, p. 245.]

CALIFORNIA.

AN ACT to prevent the importation of convicts into this State. [Passed April 11, 1850.]

The people of the State of California, represented in Senate and Assembly, do enact as follows:—

SECTION 1. No captain or master of any vessel, or any other person or persons shall, knowingly or willingly, import, bring, or send, or cause or procure to be imported, brought, or sent, or be aiding or assisting therein, into this State, by land or water, any felon, convict, or person under sentence of death or transportation, or any other legal disability incurred by a criminal prosecution, except for treason, or who shall be delivered or sent to him from any prison or place of confinement in any place without the State.

SEC. 2. Every person who shall offend against any of the provisions of the preceding section shall be deemed guilty of a misdemeanor, and, on conviction thereof, shall be punished by imprisonment in the county jail, for a term not less than three months, and shall forfeit and pay, moreover, the sum of one thousand dollars for each of such convicts so imported, brought, or sent into this State; one half of which penalty shall go to him or her who shall sue or prosecute for the same, and the other half to the county in which such prosecution shall be had.

GEORGIA.

AN ACT to prevent felons, transports from other States, coming into or residing in this. [Approved Feb. 10, 1787. Vol. 1, 234.]

IN order to prevent the dangerous evils arising from the communication with felons, transported from other States or nations, whereby the morals of many who would otherwise be good citizens may be corrupted, that from and immediately after the passing of this act, no person or persons, felons from other countries or States, transported or banished from the same for any crime or charge whatever, shall be eligible to any post, office of trust or profit, or be otherwise entitled to any of the privileges, immunities, or liberties of a freeman or freemen of this State; and on proof of the same by one legal evidence, or by the authentic certificate, under seal of any State, nation, corporation, or court, from whence he, she, or they may be banished or transported, such felon or felons shall be, by warrant and mittimus, under the hand of the chief justice of the State, or one of the justices of the court where such proof shall be established, committed to the common jail of the country, without bail or mainprize, there to remain until a convenient opportunity may be procured, by the honorable the executive, to ship or otherwise send off such felon or felons, from and without the limits of this State, never thereafter to return. And in case such felon or felons should, after such shipping or sending off, return within the limits of the same, he, she, or they shall, on conviction, suffer death without benefit of clergy: *Provided nevertheless*, on such first proof of transportation, such offender or offenders charged as felons as aforesaid shall not be debarred the right of trial by jury, and shall be allowed every right of evidence to counteract such proof. [*Cobb's Digest of* 1851, vol. 1, pp. 366, 367.]

MASSACHUSETTS.

AN ACT concerning alien passengers. [Passed May 10, 1848.]

SEC. 4. Where any vessel shall arrive at any port or harbor within this State, with alien passengers on board, who have never before been within the State, the superintendent of the city or town where it is intended to land such passengers, shall go on board such vessel, and shall examine into the condition of said passengers; and the master and commanding officer of such vessel shall, within twenty-four hours after such arrival, make a report in writing, under oath to said superintendent, of the name, age, sex, occupation, place of birth, last place of residence, and condition, of every such passenger, and none of them shall be landed, or permitted to land, until such report shall be made, except as hereinafter provided.

SEC. 5. If, on examination, there shall be found among said passengers any lunatic, idiot, maimed, aged, or infirm person, incompetent, in the opinion of the superintendent so examining, to maintain themselves, or who have been paupers in any other country, no such alien passengers shall be permitted to land until the master, owner, consignee, or agent of such vessel, shall make and deliver to said superintendent a bond to the commonwealth, with such sureties as are undoubted and satisfactory, in the sum of one thousand dollars, that no such lunatic or indigent passenger shall ever become a city, town, or State charge, from the date of said bond: *Provided, however*, That if it shall be made to appear to said superintendent, by undoubted evidence, that any passengers on board of such vessel are in such condition as to health, property, capacity, and character, that they are not likely to become chargeable to any city or town, he may permit them to be landed, on payment to him, by said master, consignee, or agent, of the sum of two dollars for each passenger so landed; and the names of all such passengers shall be certified by said superintendent on the back of the report: *And provided, further*, That if any such passengers are so sick or destitute as to require relief, and if said master shall refuse to report them, or if said master, owner, consignee, or agent, shall refuse to give such bond as is herein required, the said superintendent may permit them to be landed, and, in such cases, any city or town that shall be put to any expenses for the support, sickness, or burial, of any such passenger within ten years of the time he has so landed, may maintain an action of debt against said master, owner, consignee, or agent, and recover all expense incurred as aforesaid; and said commanding officer, owner, consignee, or agent, shall be liable to the penalties provided in the tenth section of this act.

Sec. 10. If any master or commanding officer of any vessel shall land, or permit to be landed, in this State, any alien passengers as aforesaid, without complying with the provisions of this act, said master or commanding officer, and the owner or consignee thereof, shall severally forfeit the sum of five hundred dollars for every such alien passenger so landed: *Provided always*, that the provisions in this act shall not extend to seamen sent from foreign places by consuls or vice-consuls of the United States, nor to vessels coming on shore in distress, nor to any alien passenger taken from any wreck, where life is in danger.

NEW JERSEY.

AN ACT to prevent the importation of convicts into this State. [Passed January 28, 1797.]

Sec. 1. No captain or master of any vessel, or any other person, shall knowingly or willingly import, bring, or send, or cause or procure to be imported, brought, or sent, or be aiding or assisting therein, into this state, by land or water, any felon-convict, or person convicted of an infamous crime, or under sentence of death, or any other legal disability incurred by a criminal prosecution, or who shall be delivered or sent to him or her from any prison or place of confinement, in parts out of the United States.

Sec. 2. Every captain, or master of a vessel, or other person, who shall so as aforesaid import, bring, or send, or cause or procure to be imported, brought, or sent, or be aiding or assisting therein, into this State, by land or water, or shall sell or offer for sale, any such person as above described, knowing him or her so to be, shall forfeit for every such offence two hundred dollars, to be recovered with costs by action of debt, by any person who will sue for the same, in any court of record having cognizance thereof, in which the defendant shall be ruled to give special bail, the one moiety of said forfeiture to the State, and the other moiety to the person suing for the same.

Sec. 3. Every person who shall offend against this act shall, on conviction thereof, be adjudged and ordered to enter into a recognizance, with sufficient sureties, to convey and transport, within such reasonable time as shall be directed by the court, to some place without the limits and jurisdiction of the United States, every such felon-convict, or other person of the description aforesaid, which he or she shall have been convicted of having brought, imported, or sent, or having been aiding or assisting therein, into this state, or of having so as aforesaid sold or offered for sale; and in default of entering into such recognizance, with sufficient sureties as aforesaid, he or she shall be committed to jail, there to remain without bail or mainprise, until he or she shall enter into recognizance, or shall cause such felon-convict, or other person of the description aforesaid, to be conveyed or transported to some place without the limits and jurisdiction of the United States.

PENNSYLVANIA.

ACT to prevent the landing of convicts from foreign countries. [Passed April 15, 1851.]

Be it enacted by the Senate and House of Representatives of the Commonwealth of Pennsylvania in General Assembly met, and it is hereby enacted by the authority of the same, That it shall not be lawful for the master or commander of any ship, boat or other vessel arriving from a foreign country, to bring any person, either as a passenger or hand, into any port, city, harbor, or place within this State, with intent to land or permit to land such passenger or hand, which passenger or hand shall have been or shall be a foreign convict of any felony which if committed in this State would be punished therein. Any master, commander or other officer, that shall knowingly violate this act shall, on conviction thereof in the court of quarter sessions of the county in which such offence may have been committed, be considered guilty of a misdemeanor, and subject to a fine for each offence of not less than fifty dollars nor more than three hundred dollars, or an imprisonment in the county jail for a space of not less than thirty days or more than one year, as the court may direct.

RHODE ISLAND.

AN ACT for the relief, employment, and removal of the poor.

If any master or other person having charge of any vessel shall bring into and land, or suffer to be landed in any place within this State, any person before that time convicted in any other State or in any foreign country of any infamous crime for which he hath been sentenced to transportation, knowing of such conviction or having reason to suspect it; or any person of a notoriously dissolute, infamous, and abandoned life and character, knowing him to be such, he shall for every such offence pay as a fine the sum of four hundred dollars, to and for the use of the State; to be recovered by indictments before any court of competent jurisdiction. [*Sec.* 16, *Revised Statute.*]

SOUTH CAROLINA.

AN ACT for preventing the transportation of convicted malefactors from foreign countries into this State. [Passed November 4, 1788.]

SEC. 1. *Be it enacted, &c.*, That every master or person having charge of any ship or other vessel, who shall hereafter bring into this State any convicted malefactor or person ordered for transportation for any crime or offence whatever, from any foreign country, state, or dominion, the ship or vessel bringing such persons shall be obliged to leave the port in which she shall arrive, within ten days after arrival, and shall not be permitted to take or receive on board any lading whatever, on pain of forfeiture of such ship or vessel; and if any master shall land, or suffer to be landed, or dispose of the time or service of such person, for the payment of his passage, or any other claim or demand, such master of vessel or other person having the charge thereof shall forfeit and pay for every convicted malefactor or person ordered for transportation, which such master shall bring into this State, and offer to dispose of on indenture, or other contract for service, the sum of five hundred pounds sterling.

SEC. 2. *And be it further enacted, &c.*, That every master of any vessel, or person having charge thereof, who shall bring into this State any passenger or passengers, with intent to dispose of the time of service of such passenger or passengers, for payment of his or their passage-money, or any other claim, such master of vessel shall, and he is hereby obliged to deliver, at the time of entering his vessel to the collector of the port where he shall enter, a list of all such persons whom he intends to dispose of for service, and a particular description of each, and the collector shall administer to him the following oath or affirmation, viz.:—

"I, A. B., do swear (or affirm) in the presence of Almighty God, that the passenger or passengers whom I have brought in my ship or vessel to be disposed of on service for payment of his, her, or their passage, is not, or are not, any of them, convicted malefactors, or persons ordered for transportation for any crime or offence whatever; but on the contrary, are, to the best of my information, belief, and knowledge, of good fame, character, and reputation; nor have I brought in my ship or vessel, with intent to be landed in this State, any person or persons whom I have reason to suspect is a convicted malefactor, or has been ordered for transportation for any crime whatever. So help me God."

SEC. 3. *And be it further enacted, &c.*, That if any master of any ship or other vessel shall dispose of any person for service in this State, or shall land and put on shore any passenger suspected to be a convicted malefactor, before such captain or master has made oath as aforesaid, every such captain or master of such vessel shall forfeit and pay the sum of five hundred pounds for every person who shall be disposed of or put on shore contrary to the meaning and intention of this act.

SEC. 4. *And be it further enacted, &c.,* That in case any captain or master of any ship or vessel shall not, after conviction, be able to pay the penalty inflicted by this act, he shall suffer twelve months' close imprisonment.

VIRGINIA.

IF a master of a vessel or other person, knowingly, import or bring into the State, from any place out of the United States, any person convicted of crime, or any slave sold and transported beyond the limits of this State for crime, he shall be confined in jail for three months, and be fined one hundred dollars. [*Sec.* 39, *Code of Virginia, title* 54, *chap.* 198.]

VERMONT.

IF any person shall transport any poor and indigent person, from any place without this State, to any town within this state, wherein such pauper is not lawfully settled, or aid therein, with intent to make such town chargeable with his support, he shall incur the forfeiture and liabilities imposed by the preceding section—(viz.: a sum not exceeding five hundred hundred dollars). [*Sec.* 26, *Revised Statutes, chap.* 16.]

THE following States also, namely, NEW YORK, NEW HAMPSHIRE, MAINE, MARYLAND, LOUISIANA, and TEXAS, have, each, laws relative to the introduction of immigrants, requiring of the owner, or master, or consignee of the ship or vessel landing foreign passengers, a well-secured bond to the people of the State, conditioned to indemnify and save harmless for a specified term of years every city, town, and county of the State from any cost which it may incur for the relief and support of such passengers. In lieu of such bond, commutation money may, in certain cases, be substituted. The publication of these laws is, however, omitted, since they provide no penalties with regard to the importation of paupers, convicts, lunatics, &c., similar to those contained in the laws from which extracts have been given, and are, moreover, too voluminous for the limits of this work.

LAWS OF THE UNITED STATES

RELATIVE TO THE

CARRIAGE OF PASSENGERS IN PASSENGER-SHIPS AND VESSELS.

THE first Act of Congress "regulating passenger-ships and vessels," was approved March 2, 1819.

By this Act, a passenger-ship or vessel was allowed to carry two passengers, and not more than two, to every five tons of her measurement according to the customhouse rule.

A second Act, approved February 22, 1847, allowed to each passenger "fourteen clear superficial feet of deck" on the lower deck or platform, if such vessel were not to pass within the tropics during the voyage: but if such vessel were to pass within the tropics during the voyage, then "twenty such clear superficial feet of deck" were allotted to each passenger: and, to each passenger on the orlop deck (if any) "thirty such superficial feet in all cases." Such space, occupied by passengers and appropriated for their use, was to be unoccupied by stores or other goods, not being the personal luggage of such passengers.

Such ship or vessel to have not more than two tiers of berths: the berths to be well constructed, and to be at least six feet in length and eighteen inches in width for each passenger.

Children under the age of one year not to be included in the computation of the number of passengers.

Two children, each under the age of eight years, to be estimated as equal to one passenger.

A third Act was approved March 2, 1847. So much of the second Act as authorizes shippers, in the assignment of room, to estimate two children of eight years of age and under as equal to one passenger was, by this Act, repealed.

A fourth Act, regulating the transportation of colored emigrants from the United States to the coast of Africa, was approved January 31, 1848. It contained, however, no provision relating to the bringing of immigrants to this country.

A fifth Act, "to provide for the ventilation of passenger-vessels, and for other purposes," was approved May 17, 1848.

In the framing of the previous acts, the comfort and health of the passengers do not seem to have been specially consulted. In this Act, however, there were several humane provisions.

It provided for a more complete ventilation of the vessel.

It prescribed the quantity of supplies of provisions, water, and fuel.

It established cooking-ranges for the use of the passengers.

It made it the duty of the captain to cause the apartment occupied by the passengers to be kept, at all times, in a clean and healthy state.

It amended the Act of February 22, 1847, so that, instead of fourteen feet, as prescribed in said Act, sixteen clear superficial feet should be allowed to each passenger, if the distance between decks were less than six feet and not less than five feet: and if less than five feet, then twenty-two clear superficial feet were allotted to each passenger: and it repealed so much of former laws as limited the number of passengers to two for every five tons.

A sixth Act was approved March 3, 1849.

It required the owners and masters of passenger-vessels to furnish to each passenger the daily supply of water mentioned in the fourth Section of the Act of May 17, 1848; but repealed the allowance of food and fuel prescribed therein, and only required of such owners and masters to "furnish, or cause the passengers to furnish for themselves, a sufficient supply of good and wholesome food."

It amended the Act of February 22, 1847, so that a vessel passing into or through the tropics should be allowed to carry the same number of passengers as vessels that did not enter the tropics.

This Act, so far as it permitted passengers to "furnish for themselves a sufficient supply of good and wholesome food," was ill-advised, inasmuch as it is well known that immigrants, in order to avoid expense, have, not unfrequently, subsisted on the scantiest fare during the voyage, while the owners and masters of such vessels remained in ignorance of the fact.

Health and strength are desirable elements in the character of immigration, and immigrants, on reaching our shores, should not be wasted by sickness nor weakened by hunger.

This truth seems to have been considered in the framing of the seventh, and last "Act to regulate the carriage of passengers in steamships and other vessels," approved March 3, 1855. By this Act all former laws regulating the carriage of passengers in passenger-ships and vessels are expressly repealed, and new regulations in regard to the same are instituted.

These Acts are herewith published in full, and in the order of their approval. Annexed to them will be found "General Regulations, No. 45," issued to Collectors and other officers of the customs, by the Treasury Department, under the Passenger-Act now in force.

AN ACT regulating passenger-ships and vessels.

SEC. 1. *Be it enacted by the Senate and House of Representatives of the United States of America in Congress assembled,* That, if the master or other person on board of any ship or vessel, owned in the whole or in part by a citizen or citizens of the United States, or the territories thereof, or by a subject or subjects, citizen or citizens, of any foreign country, shall, after the first day of January next, take on board of such ship or vessel, at any foreign port or place, or shall bring or convey into the United States, or the territories thereof, from any foreign port or place; or shall carry, convey, or transport, from the United States, or the territories thereof, to any foreign port or place, a greater number of passengers than two for every five tons of such ship or vessel, according to customhouse measurement, every such master, or other person so offending, and the owner or owners of such ship or vessel, shall severally forfeit and pay to the United States the sum of one hundred and fifty dollars, for each and every passenger so taken on board of such ship or vessel over and above the aforesaid number of two to every five tons of such ship or vessel; to be recovered by suit in any circuit or district court of the United States, where the said vessel may arrive, or where the owner or owners aforesaid may reside: *Provided, nevertheless,* That nothing in this act shall be taken to apply to the complement of men usually and ordinarily employed in navigating such ship or vessel.

SEC. 2. That if the number of passengers so taken on board of any ship or vessel as aforesaid, or conveyed or brought into the United States, or transported therefrom as aforesaid, shall exceed the said proportion of two to every five tons of such ship or vessel, by the number of twenty passengers, in the whole, every such ship or vessel shall be deemed and taken to be forfeited to the United States, and shall be prosecuted and distributed in the same manner in which the forfeitures and penalties are recovered and distributed under the provisions of the act, entitled "An act to regulate the collection of duties on imports and tonnage."

SEC. 3. That every ship or vessel bound on a voyage from the United States to any port on the continent of Europe, at the time of leaving the last port whence such ship or vessel shall sail, shall have on board, well secured under deck, at least sixty gallons of water, one hundred pounds of salted provisions, one gallon of vinegar, and one hundred pounds of wholesome ship bread, for each and every passenger on board such ship or vessel, over and above such other provisions, stores, and live stock, as may be put on board by such master or passenger for their use, or that of the crew of such ship or vessel; and in like proportion for a shorter or longer voyage; and if the passengers, on board of such ship or vessel in which the proportion of provisions herein directed shall not have been provided, shall at any time be put on short allowance, in water, flesh, vinegar, or bread, during any voyage aforesaid, the master and owner of such ship or vessel shall, severally, pay, to each and every passenger who shall have been put on short allowance as aforesaid, the sum of three dollars for each and every day they may have been on such short allowance; to be recovered in the same manner as seamen's wages are or may be recovered.

SEC. 4. That the captain or master of any ship or vessel arriving in the United States, or any of the territories thereof, from any foreign place whatever, at the same time that he delivers a manifest of the cargo, and, if there be no cargo, then at the time of making report or entry of the ship or vessel, pursuant to the existing laws of the United States, shall also deliver and report, to the collector of the district in which such ship or vessel shall arrive, a list or manifest of all the passengers taken on board of the said ship or vessel at any foreign port or place in which list or manifest it shall be the duty of the said master to designate, particularly, the age, sex, and occupation, of the said passengers, respectively, the country to which they severally belong, and that of which it is their intention to become inhabitants; and shall further set forth whether any, and what number, have died on the voyage; which report and manifest shall be sworn to by the said master, in the same manner as is directed by the existing laws of the United States in relation to the manifest of the cargo; and that the refusal or neglect of the master aforesaid to comply with the provisions of this section, shall incur the same penalties, disabilities, and forfeitures, as are at present provided for a refusal or neglect to report and deliver a manifest of the cargo aforesaid.

SEC. 5. That each and every collector of the customs, to whom such manifest or list of passengers aforesaid shall be delivered, shall, quarter-yearly, return copies thereof to the Secretary of State of the United States, by whom statements of the same shall be laid before Congress at each and every session.

Approved, March 2, 1819.

AN ACT to regulate the carriage of passengers in merchant-vessels.

SEC. 1. *Be it enacted by the Senate and House of Representatives of the United States of America, in Congress assembled,* That if the master of any vessel, owned in whole or in part by a citizen of the United States of America, or by a citizen of any foreign country, shall take on board such vessel, at any foreign port or place, a greater number of passengers than in the following proportion to the space occupied by them and appropriated for their use, and unoccupied by stores or other goods, not being the personal luggage of such passengers, that is to say, on the lower deck or platform one passenger for every fourteen clear superficial feet of deck, if such vessel is not to pass within the tropics during such voyage; but if such vessel is to pass within the tropics during such voyage, then one passenger for every twenty such clear superficial feet of deck, and on the orlop deck (if any) one passenger for every thirty superficial feet in all cases, with intent to bring such passengers to the United States of America, and shall leave such port or place with the same, and bring the same, or any number thereof, within the jurisdiction of the United States aforesaid, or if any such master of a vessel shall take on board of his vessel at any port or place within the jurisdiction of the United States aforesaid any greater number of passengers than the proportions aforesaid admit, with intent to carry the same to any foreign port or place, every such master shall be deemed guilty of a misdemeanor, and, upon conviction thereof, before any circuit or district court of the United States aforesaid, shall, for each passenger taken on board beyond the above proportions, be fined in the sum of fifty dollars, and may also be imprisoned for any term not exceeding one year: *Provided,* That this act shall not be construed to permit any ship or vessel, to carry more than two passengers to five tons of such ship or vessel.

SEC. 2. *And be it further enacted,* That if the passengers so taken on board of such vessel, and brought into or transported from the United States aforesaid, shall exceed the number limited by the last section to the number of twenty in the whole, such vessel shall be forfeited to the United States aforesaid, and be prosecuted and distributed as forfeitures are, under the act to regulate duties on imports and tonnage.

SEC. 3. *And be it further enacted,* That if any such vessel as aforesaid shall have more than two tiers of berths, or in case, in such vessel, the interval between the floor and the deck or platform beneath shall not be at least six inches, and the berths well constructed; or in case the dimensions of such berths shall not be at least six feet in length, and at least eighteen inches in width, for each passenger as aforesaid, then the master of said vessel, and the owners thereof, severally, shall forfeit and pay the sum of five dollars for each and every passenger on board of said vessel on such voyage, to be recovered by the United States as aforesaid in any circuit or district court of the United States where such vessel may arrive, or from which she sails.

SEC. 4. *And be it further enacted,* That, for the purposes of this act, it shall in all cases be computed that two children each being under the age of eight years, shall be equal to one passenger, and that children under the age of one year shall not be included in the computation of the number of passengers.

SEC. 5. *And be it further enacted,* That the amount of the several penalties imposed by this act shall be liens on the vessel or vessels violating its provisions; and such vessel may be libelled and sold therefor in the district court of the United States aforesaid in which such vessel shall arrive.

Approved, February 22, 1847.

AN ACT to amend an act entitled, "An act to regulate the carriage of passengers in merchant-vessels," and to determine the time when said act shall take effect.

SEC. 1. *Be it enacted by the Senate and House of Representatives of the United States of America in Congress assembled,* That the act to regulate the carriage of passengers in merchant-vessels, approved the twenty-second day of February, eighteen hundred and forty-seven, shall, in regard to all vessels arriving from ports on this side of the Capes of Good Hope and Horn, take effect and be in force from and after the thirty-first day of May next ensuing; and in regard to all vessels arriving from places beyond said capes, on and after the thirtieth day of October next ensuing.

SEC. 2. *And be it further enacted,* That so much of said act as authorized shippers to estimate two children of eight years of age and under as one passenger, in the assignment of room, is hereby repealed.

Approved, March 2, 1847.

AN ACT exempting vessels employed by the American Colonization Society in transporting colored emigrants from the United States to the coast of Africa, from the provisions of the acts of the twenty-second of February and second of March, eighteen hundred and forty-seven, regulating the carriage of passengers in merchant-vessels.

Be it enacted by the Senate and House of Representatives of the United States of America in Congress assembled, That, from and after the passage of this act, all and every vessel which shall or may be employed by the American Colonization Society, or by the Maryland State Colonization Society, to transport, and which shall actually transport, from any port or ports in the United States to any colony or colonies on the west coast of Africa, colored emigrants to reside there, shall be, and the same are hereby, excepted out of and exempted from the operation of the act entitled, "An act to regulate the carriage of passengers in merchant-vessels," passed twenty-second February, eighteen hundred and forty-seven; and of the act entitled, "An act to amend an act entitled, 'An act to regulate the carriage of passengers in merchant-vessels, and to determine the time when such act shall take effect,'" passed second March, eighteen hundred and forty-seven.

Approved, January 31, 1848.

AN ACT to provide for the ventilation of passenger-vessels, and for other purposes.

Be it enacted by the Senate and House of Representatives of the United States of America in Congress assembled, That all vessels, whether of the United States or any other country, having sufficient capacity, according to law, for fifty or more passengers (other than cabin passengers), shall, when employed in transporting such passengers between the United States and Europe, have on the upper deck, for the use of such passengers, a house over the passage-way leading to the apartment allotted to such passengers below deck, firmly secured to the deck or combings of the hatch, with two doors, the sills of which shall be at least one foot above the deck, so constructed that one door or window in such house may at all times be left open for ventilation; and all vessels so employed, and having the capacity to carry one hundred and fifty such passengers or more, shall have two such houses, and the stairs, or ladder, leading down to the aforesaid apartment shall be furnished with a hand-rail of wood or strong rope: *Provided, nevertheless,* booby-hatches may be substituted for such houses in vessels having three permanent decks.

SEC. 2. *And be it further enacted,* That every such vessel so employed, and having the legal capacity for more than one hundred such passengers, shall have at least two ventilators to purify the apartment or apartments occupied by such passengers—one of which shall be inserted in the after part of the apartment or apartments, and the other shall be placed in the forward portion of the apartment or apartments, and one of them shall have an exhausting cap to carry off the foul air, and the other a receiving cap to carry down the fresh air; which said ventilations shall have a capacity proportioned to the size of the apartment or apartments to be purified, namely, if the apartment or apartments will lawfully authorize the reception of two hundred such passengers, the capacity of such ventilators shall, each of them, be equal to a tube of twelve inches diameter in the clear, and in proportion for larger or smaller apartments; and all said ventilators shall rise at least four feet six inches above the upper deck of any such vessel, and be of the most approved form and construction: *Provided,* That if it shall appear, from the report to be made and approved, as provided in the seventh section of this act, that such vessel is equally well ventilated by any other means, such other means of ventilation shall be deemed, and held to be, a compliance with the provisions of this section.

SEC. 3. *And be it further enacted,* That every vessel carrying more than fifty such passengers shall have for their use on deck, housed and conveniently arranged, at least one camboose or cooking range, the dimensions of which shall be equal to four feet long and one foot six inches wide for every two hundred passengers, and provision shall be made in the manner aforesaid in this ratio for a greater or less number of passengers: *Provided, however,* And nothing herein contained shall take away the right to make such arrangements for cooking between decks, if that shall be deemed desirable.

SEC. 4. *And be it further enacted,* That all vessels employed as aforesaid shall have on board, for the use of such passengers, at the time of leaving the last port whence such vessel shall sail, well secured under deck, for each passenger, at least fifteen pounds of good navy bread, ten pounds of rice, ten pounds of oat-meal, ten pounds of wheat-flour, ten pounds of peas and beans, thirty-five pounds of potatoes, one pint of vinegar, sixty gallons of fresh water, ten pounds of salted pork, free of bone, all to be of good quality, and a sufficient supply of fuel for cooking; but at places where either rice, oat-meal, wheat-flour, or peas and beans, can not be procured, of good quality, and on reasonable terms, the quantity of either or any of the other last-named articles may be increased and substituted therefor; and in case potatoes can not be procured on reasonable terms, one pound of either of said articles may be substituted in lieu of five pounds of potatoes; and the captains of such vessels shall deliver to each passenger at least one tenth part of the aforesaid provisions weekly, commencing on the day of sailing; and daily at least three quarts of water, and sufficient fuel for cooking; and if the passengers on board of any such vessel in which the provisions, fuel, and water, herein required, shall not have been provided as aforesaid, shall, at any time, be put on short allowance during any voyage, the master or owner of any such vessels shall pay to each and every passenger, who shall have been put on short allowance, the sum of three dollars for each and every day they may have been on such short allowance, to be recovered in the circuit or district court of the United States: *Provided, nevertheless*, and nothing herein contained shall prevent any passenger, with the consent of the captain, from furnishing for himself the articles of food herein specified, and, if put on board in good order, it shall fully satisfy the provisions of this act so far as regards food: *And provided, further*, That any passenger may also, with the consent of the captain, furnish for himself an equivalent for the articles of food required in other and different articles; and if without waste or neglect on the part of the passenger or inevitable accident, they prove insufficient, and the captain shall furnish comfortable food to such passengers during the residue of the voyage, this in regard to food shall also be a compliance with the terms of this act.

SEC. 5. *And be it further enacted*, That the captain of any such vessel so employed is hereby authorized to maintain good discipline, and such habits of cleanliness among such passengers as will tend to the preservation and promotion of health; and to that end, he shall cause such regulations as he may adopt for this purpose to be posted up before sailing, on board such vessel, in a place accessible to such passengers, and shall keep the same so posted up during the voyage; and it is hereby made the duty of said captain to cause the apartment occupied by such passengers to be kept, at all times, in a clean, healthy state; and the owners of every such vessel so employed are required to construct the decks, and all parts of said apartment, so that it can be thoroughly cleansed; and they shall also provide a safe and convenient privy or water-closet for the exclusive use of every one hundred such passengers. And when the weather is such that said passengers can not be mustered on deck with their bedding, it shall be the duty of the captain of every such vessel to cause the deck occupied by such passengers to be cleaned [cleansed] with chloride of lime, or some other equally efficient disinfecting agent, and also at such other times as said captain may deem necessary.

SEC. 6. *And be it further enacted,* That the master and owner or owners of any such vessel so employed, which shall not be provided with the house or houses over the passage-ways, as prescribed in the first section of this act; or with ventilators, as prescribed in the second section of this act; or with the camboose or cooking-ranges, with the houses over them, as prescribed in the third section of this act; shall severally forfeit and pay to the United States the sum of two hundred dollars for each and every violation of, or neglect to conform to, the provisions of each of said sections; and fifty dollars for each and every neglect or violation of any of the provisions of the fifth section of this act; to be recovered by suit in any circuit or district court of the United States, within the jurisdiction of which the said vessel may arrive, or from which it may be about to depart, or at any place within the jurisdiction of such courts, wherever the owner or owners, or captain of such vessel, may be found.

SEC. 7. *And be it further enacted,* That the collector of the customs, at any port in the United States at which any vessel so employed shall arrive, or from which any such vessel shall be about to depart, shall appoint and direct one of the inspectors of the customs for such port to examine such vessel, and report in writing to such collector, whether the provisions of the first, second, third, and fifth sections of this act have been complied with in respect to such vessel; and if such report shall state such compliance, and be approved by such collector, it shall be deemed and held as conclusive evidence thereof.

SEC. 8. *And be it further enacted,* That the first section of an act entitled, "An act to regulate the carriage of passengers in merchant-vessels," approved February twenty-second, eighteen hundred and forty-seven, be so amended, that when the height or distance between the decks of the vessels referred to in the said section, shall be less than six feet, and not less than five feet, there shall be allowed to each passenger sixteen clear superficial feet on the deck, instead of fourteen, as prescribed in said section; and if the height or distance between the decks shall be less than five feet, there shall be allowed to each passenger twenty-two clear superficial feet on deck: and if the master of any such vessel, shall take on board his vessel, in any port of the United States, a greater number of passengers than is allowed by this section, with the intent specified in said first section of the act of eighteen hundred and forty-seven, or if the master of any such vessel shall take on board, at a foreign port, and bring within the jurisdiction of the United States, a greater number of passengers than is allowed by this section, such master shall be deemed guilty of a misdemeanor, and upon conviction thereof shall be punished in the manner provided for the punishment of persons convicted of a violation of the act aforesaid; and in computing the number of passengers on board such vessels, all children under the age of one year, at the time of embarkation, shall be excluded from such computation.

Sec. 9. *And be it further enacted*, That this act shall take effect, in respect to such vessels sailing from ports in the United States, in thirty days from the time of its approval; and in respect to every such vessel sailing from ports in Europe, in sixty days after such approval; and it is hereby made the duty of the Secretary of State to give notice, in the ports of Europe, of this act, in such manner as he may deem proper.

Sec. 10. *And be it further enacted*, That so much of the first section of the act entitled, "An act regulating passenger-ships and vessels," approved March second, eighteen hundred and nineteen, or any other act that limits the number of passenger to two for every five tons, is hereby repealed.

Approved, May 17, 1848.

AN ACT to extend the provisions of all laws now in force relating to the carriage of passengers in merchant-vessels, and the regulation thereof.

Sec. 1. *Be it enacted by the Senate and House of Representatives of the United States of America, in Congress assembled*, That all vessels bound from any port in the United States to any port or place in the Pacific ocean, or on its tributaries, or from any such port or place to any port in the United States on the Atlantic or its tributaries, shall be subject to the provisions of all the laws now in force relating to the carriage of passengers in merchant-vessels sailing to and from foreign countries, and the regulation thereof, except the fourth section of the "Act to provide for the ventilation of passenger-vessels, and for other purposes," approved May seventeenth, eighteen hundred and forty-eight, relating to provisions, water, and fuel; but the owners and masters of all such vessels shall in all cases furnish to each passenger the daily supply of water therein mentioned, and they shall furnish, or cause the passengers to furnish for themselves, a sufficient supply of good and wholesome food; and in case they shall fail so to do, or shall provide unwholesome or unsuitable provisions, they shall be subject to the penalty provided in said fourth section in case passengers are put on short allowance of water or provisions.

Sec. 2. *And be it further enacted*, That the act entitled, "An act to regulate the carriage of passengers in merchant-vessels," approved February 22, 1847, shall be so amended as that a vessel passing into or through the tropics shall be allowed to carry the same number of passengers as vessels that do not enter the tropics.

Sec. 3. *And be it further enacted*, That this act shall take effect on and after the fifteenth day of March, eighteen hundred and forty-nine.

Approved, March 3, 1849.

AN ACT to regulate the carriage of passengers in steamships and other vessels.

Be it enacted by the Senate and House of Representatives of the United States of America in Congress assembled, That no master of any vessel owned in whole or in part by a citizen of the United States, or by a citizen of any foreign country, shall take on board such vessel, at any foreign port or place, other than foreign contiguous territory of the United States, a greater number of passengers than in proportion of one to every two tons of such vessel, not including children under the age of one year in the computation, and computing two children over one and under eight years of age as one passenger. That the spaces appropriated for the use of such passengers, and which shall not be occupied by stores or other goods not being the personal baggage of such passengers, shall be in the following proportions, viz.: On the main and poop decks or platforms and in the deck houses, if there be any, one passenger for each sixteen clear superficial feet of deck, if the height or distance between the decks or platforms shall not be less than six feet; and on the lower deck (not being an orlop deck), if any, one passenger for eighteen such clear superficial feet, if the height or distance between the decks or platforms shall not be less than six feet, but so as that no passenger shall be carried on any other deck or platform, nor upon any deck where the height or distance between decks is less than six feet, with intent to bring such passenger to the United States, and shall leave such port or place and bring the same, or any number thereof, within the jurisdiction of the United States; or if any such master of any vessel shall take on board his vessel, at any port or place within the jurisdiction of the United States, any greater number of passengers than in the proportion aforesaid to the space aforesaid, or to the tonnage aforesaid, with intent to carry the same to any foreign port or place other than foreign contiguous territory as aforesaid, every such master shall be deemed guilty of a misdemeanor, and, upon conviction thereof, before any circuit or district court of the United States shall, for each passenger taken on board beyond the limit aforesaid, or the space aforesaid, be fined in the sum of fifty dollars, and may also be imprisoned, at the discretion of the judge before whom the penalty shall be recovered, not exceeding six months; but should it be necessary for the safety or convenience of the vessel, that any portion of her cargo or any other articles, or article, should be placed on, or stored in, any of the decks, cabins, or other places appropriated to the use of passengers, the same may be placed in lockers or enclosures prepared for the purpose, on an exterior surface impervious to the wave, capable of being cleansed in like manner as the decks or platforms of the vessel. In no case, however, shall the places thus provided be deemed to be a part of the space allowable for the use of passengers, but the same shall be deducted therefrom, and in all cases where prepared or used, the upper surface of said lockers on enclosed spaces shall be deemed and taken to be the deck or platform from which measurement shall be made for all the purposes of this act. It is also provided that one hospital in the spaces appropriated to passengers, and separate therefrom by an appropriate partition, and furnished as its purposes require, may be prepared, and, when used, may be included in the space allowable for passengers, but the same shall not occupy more than one hundred superficial feet of deck or platform: *Provided*, That on board two-deck ships, where the height between the decks is seven and one half feet or more, fourteen clear superficial feet of deck shall be the proportion required for each passenger.

SEC. 2. *And be it further enacted*, That no such vessel shall have more than two tiers of berths, and the interval between the lowest part thereof and the deck or platform beneath, shall not be less than nine inches, and the berths shall be well constructed, parallel with the sides of the vessel, and separated from each other by partitions, as berths ordinarily are separated, and shall be at least six feet in length and at least two feet in width, and each berth shall be occupied by no more than one passenger; but double berths of twice the above width may be constructed, each berth to be occupied by no more, and by no other, than two women, or by one woman and two children under the age of eight years, or by husband and wife, or by a man and two of his own children under the age of eight years, or by two men, members of the same family; and if there shall be any violation of this section in any of its provisions, then the master of the vessel and the owners thereof shall severally forfeit and pay the sum of five dollars for each passenger on board of such vessel on such voyage, to be recovered by the United States in any port where such vessel may arrive or depart.

SEC. 3. *And be it further enacted*, That all vessels, whether of the United States or any foreign country, having sufficient capacity or space according to law for fifty or more passengers (other than cabin passengers) shall, when employed in transporting such passengers between the United States and Europe, have, on the upper deck, for the use of such passengers, a house over the passage-way leading to the apartments allotted to such passengers below deck, firmly secured to the deck or combings of the hatch, with two doors, the sills of which shall be at least one foot above the deck, so constructed that one door or window in such house may at all times be left open for ventilation; and all vessels so employed, and having the capacity to carry one hundred and fifty such passengers or more, shall have two such houses; and the stairs or ladder leading down to the aforesaid apartment shall be furnished with a hand-rail of wood or strong rope; but booby-hatches may be substituted for such houses.

SEC. 4. *And be it further enacted*, That every such vessel so employed, and having the legal capacity for more than one hundred such passengers, shall have at least two ventilators to purify the apartment or apartments occupied by such passengers; one of which shall be inserted in the after part of the apartment or apartments, and the other shall be placed in the forward portion of the apartment or apartments, and one of them shall have an exhausting cap to carry off the foul air, and the other a receiving cap to carry down the fresh air; which said ventilators shall have a capacity proportioned to the size of the apartment or apartments to be purified, namely: if the apartment or apartments will lawfully authorize the reception of two hundred such passengers, the capacity of such ventilators shall each be equal to a tube of twelve inches diameter in the clear, and in proportion for larger or smaller apartments; and all said ventilators shall rise at least four feet six inches above the upper deck of any such vessel, and be of the most approved form and construction; but if it shall appear, from the report, to be made and approved, as hereinafter provided, that such vessel is equally well ventilated by any other means, such other means of ventilation shall be deemed and held to be a compliance with the provisions of this section.

SEC. 5. *And be it further enacted,* That every vessel carrying more than fifty such passengers shall have for their use on deck, housed and conveniently arranged, at least one camboose or cooking-range, the dimensions of which shall be equal to four feet long and one foot six inches wide for every two hundred passengers; and provision shall be made in the manner aforesaid, in this ratio, for a greater or less number of passengers; but nothing herein contained shall take away the right to make such arrangements for cooking between decks, if that shall be deemed desirable.

SEC. 6. *And be it further enacted,* That all vessels employed as aforesaid shall have on board, for the use of such passengers, at the time of leaving the last port whence such vessel shall sail, well secured under deck, for each passenger, at least twenty pounds of good navy bread, fifteen pounds of rice, fifteen pounds of oat-meal, ten pounds of wheat-flour, fifteen pounds of peas and beans, twenty pounds of potatoes, one pint of vinegar, sixty gallons of fresh water, ten pounds of salted pork, ten pounds of salt beef, free of bones, all to be of good quality; but at places where either rice, oat-meal, wheat-flour, or peas and beans, can not be procured, of good quality, and on reasonable terms, the quantity of either or any of the other last-named articles may be increased and substituted therefor; and in case potatoes can not be procured on reasonable terms, one pound of either of said articles may be substituted in lieu of five pounds of potatoes; and the captains of such vessels shall deliver to each passenger at least one tenth part of the aforesaid provisions weekly, commencing on the day of sailing, and at least three quarts of water daily; and if the passengers on board of any such vessel in which the provisions and water herein required shall not have been provided as aforesaid, shall at any time be put on short allowance during any voyage, the master or owner of any such vessels shall pay to each and every passenger who shall have been put on short allowance, the sum of three dollars for each and every day they may have been put on short allowance, to be recovered in the circuit or district court of the United States: and it shall be the duty of the captain or master of every such ship or vessel, to cause the food and provisions of all the passengers to be well and properly cooked daily, and to be served out and distributed to them at regular and stated hours by messes, or in such other manner as shall be deemed best and most conducive to the health and comfort of such passengers, of which hours and manner of distribution, due and sufficient notice shall be given. If the captain or master of any such ship or vessel shall wilfully fail to furnish and distribute such provisions cooked as aforesaid, he shall be deemed guilty of a misdemeanor, and, upon conviction thereof before any circuit or district court of the United States, shall be fined not more than one thousand dollars, and shall be imprisoned for a term not exceeding one year: *Provided*, That the enforcement of this penalty shall not affect the civil responsibility of the captain or master and owners to such passengers as may have suffered from said default.

SEC. 7. *And be it further enacted*, That the captain of any such vessel so employed is hereby authorized to maintain good discipline, and such habits of cleanliness among such passengers as will tend to the preservation and promotion of health; and to that end, he shall cause such regulations as he may adopt for this purpose, to be posted up, before sailing, on board such vessel, in a place accessible to such passengers, and shall keep the same so posted up during the voyage; and it is hereby made the duty of said captain to cause the apartments occupied by such passengers to be kept at all times in a clean, healthy state; and the owners of every such vessel so employed are required to construct the decks, and all parts of said apartment, so that it can be thoroughly cleansed; and they shall also provide a safe, convenient privy or water-closet for the exclusive use of every one hundred such passengers. And when the weather is such that said passengers can not be mustered on deck with their bedding, it shall be the duty of the captain of every such vessel to cause the deck occupied by such passengers to be cleansed with chloride of lime, or some other equally efficient disinfecting agent, and also at such other times as said captain may deem necessary.

SEC. 8. *And be it further enacted*, That the master and owner or owners of any such vessel so employed, which shall not be provided with the house or houses over the passage-ways, as prescribed in the third section of this chapter, or with ventilators, as prescribed in the fourth section of this chapter, or with the camobooses or cooking-ranges, with the houses over them, as prescribed in the fifth section of this chapter, shall severally forfeit and pay to the United States the sum of two hundred dollars for each and every violation of, or neglect to conform to, the provisions of each of said sections; and fifty dollars for each and every neglect or violation of any of the provisions of the seventh section of this chapter, to be recovered by suit in any circuit or district court of the United States, within the jurisdiction of which the said vessel may arrive, or from which she may be about to depart, or at any place within the jurisdiction of such courts, wherever the owner or owners or captain of such vessel may be found.

SEC. 9. *And be it further enacted,* That the collector of the customs, at any port of the United States at which any vessel so employed shall arrive, or from which any such vessel shall be about to depart, shall appoint and direct one or more of the inspectors of the customs for such port to examine such vessel, and report, in writing, to such collector, whether the requirements of law have been complied with in respect to such vessel; and if such report shall state such compliance, and shall be approved by such collector, it shall be deemed and held as prima-facie evidence thereof.

SEC. 10. *And be it further enacted,* That the provisions, requisitions, penalties, and liens of this act, relating to the space in vessels appropriated to the use of passengers, are hereby extended and made applicable to all spaces appropriated to the use of steerage passengers in vessels propelled in whole or in part by steam, and navigating from, to, and between the ports, and in manner as in this act named, and to such vessels and to the masters thereof; and so much of the act entitled, "An act to amend an act entitled, 'An act to provide for the better security of the lives of passengers on board of vessels propelled in whole or in part by steam, and for other purposes,'" approved August thirtieth, eighteen hundred and fifty-two, as conflicts with this act, is hereby repealed; and the space appropriated to the use of steerage passengers in vessels so as above propelled and navigated, is hereby subject to the supervision and inspection of the collector of the customs in any port of the United States at which any such vessel shall arrive, or from which she shall be about to depart; and the same shall be examined and reported in the same manner, and by the same officers, by the next preceding section directed to examine and report.

SEC. 11. *And be it further enacted,* That the vessels bound from any port in the United States to any port or place in the Pacific ocean, or on its tributaries, or from any such port or place to any port in the United States on the Atlantic or its tributaries, shall be subject to the foregoing provisions regulating the carriage of passengers in merchant-vessels, except so much as relates to provisions and water; but the owners and masters of all such vessels shall in all cases furnish to each passenger the daily supply of water therein mentioned, and they shall furnish a sufficient supply of good and wholesome food, properly cooked; and in case they shall fail so to do, or shall provide unwholesome or unsuitable provisions, they shall be subject to the penalty provided in the sixth section of this chapter, in case the passengers are put on short allowance of water or provisions.

SEC. 12. *And be it further enacted,* That the captain or master of any ship or vessel arriving in the United States, or any of the territories thereof, from any foreign place whatever, at the same time that he delivers a manifest of the cargo, and if there be no cargo, then at the time of making report or entry of the ship or vessel, pursuant to law, shall also deliver and report to the collector of the district in which such ship or vessel shall arrive, a list or manifest of all the passengers taken on board of the said ship or vessel at any foreign port or place; in which list or manifest it shall be the duty of the said master to designate, particularly, the age, sex, and occupation of the said passengers, respectively, the part of the vessel occupied by each during the voyage, the country to which they severally belong, and that of which it is their intention to become inhabitants; and shall further set forth whether any, and what number, have died on the voyage; which list or manifest shall be sworn to by the said master, in the same manner as directed by law in relation to the manifest of the cargo, and the refusal or neglect of the master aforesaid to comply with the provisions of this section, or any part thereof, shall incur the same penalties, disabilities, and forfeitures, as are provided for a refusal or neglect to report and deliver a manifest of the cargo aforesaid.

SEC. 13. *And be it further enacted,* That each and every collector of the customs, to whom such manifest or list of passengers as aforesaid shall be delivered, shall quarter-yearly return copies thereof to the Secretary of State of the United States, by whom statements of the same shall be laid before Congress at each and every session.

SEC. 14. *And be it further enacted,* That in case there shall have occurred on board any ship or vessel arriving at any port or place within the United States or its territories, any death or deaths among the passengers (other than cabin passengers), the master or captain or owner or consignee of such ship or vessel, shall, within twenty-four hours after the time within which the report and list or manifest of passengers mentioned in section twelve of this act is required to be delivered to the collector of the customs, pay to the said collector the sum of ten dollars for each and every passenger above the age of eight years who shall have died on the voyage, by natural disease; and the said collector shall pay the money thus received, at such times and in such manner as the Secretary of the Treasury, by general rules, shall direct, to any board or commission appointed by, and acting under the authority of, the State within which the port where such ship or vessel arrived is situated, for the care and protection of sick, indigent, or destitute immigrants, to be applied to the objects of their appointment; and if there be more than one board or commission who shall claim such payment, the Secretary of the Treasury, for the time being, shall determine which is entitled to receive the same, and his decision in the premises shall be final and without appeal: *Provided,* That the payment shall in no case be awarded or made to any board or commission or association formed for the protection or advancement of any particular class of immigrants, or immigrants of any particular nation or creed, and if the master, captain, owner, or consignee of any ship or vessel, refuse or neglect to pay to the collector the sum and sums of money required, and within the time prescribed by this section, he or they shall severally forfeit and pay the sum of fifty dollars in addition to such sum of ten dollars for each and every passenger upon whose death the same has become payable, to be recovered by the United States in any circuit or district court of the United States where such vessel may arrive, or such master, captain, owner, or consignee, may reside; and when recovered, the said money shall be disposed of in the same manner as is directed with respect to the sum and sums required to be paid to the collector of customs.

SEC. 15. *And be it further enacted,* That the amount of the several penalties imposed by the foregoing provisions regulating the carriage of passengers in merchant-vessels, shall be liens on the vessel or vessels violating those provisions, and such vessel or vessels shall be libelled therefor in any circuit or district court of the United States where such vessel or vessels shall arrive.

SEC. 16. *And be it further enacted,* That all and every vessel or vessels which shall or may be employed by the American Colonization Society, or the Colonization Society of any State, to transport, and which shall actually transport, from any port or ports of the United States to any colony or colonies on the west coast of Africa, colored emigrants to reside there, shall be, and the same are hereby, subjected to the operation of the foregoing provisions regulating the carriage of passengers in merchant-vessels.

SEC. 17. *And be it further enacted,* That the collector of the customs shall examine each immigrant ship or vessel on its arrival at his port, and ascertain and report to the Secretary of the Treasury the time of sailing, the length of the voyage, the ventilation, the number of passengers, their space on board, their food, the native country of the immigrants, the number of deaths, the age and sex of those who died during the voyage; together with his opinion of the cause of the mortality, if any, on board, and, if none, what precautionary measures, arrangements, or habits, are supposed to have had any, and what, agency in causing the exemption.

SEC. 18. *And be it further enacted,* That this act shall take effect, with respect to vessels sailing from ports in the United States on the eastern side of the continent, within thirty days from the time of its approval; and with respect to vessels sailing from ports in the United States on the western side of the continent, and from ports in Europe, within sixty days from the time of its approval; and with respect to vessels sailing from ports in other parts of the world, within six months from the time of its approval.

And it is hereby made the duty of the Secretary of State to give notice, in the ports of Europe and elsewhere, of this act, in such manner as he shall deem proper.

SEC. 19. *And be it further enacted,* That from and after the time that this act shall take effect with respect to any vessels, then in respect to such vessels, the act of second March, eighteen hundred and nineteen, entitled, "An act regulating passenger-ships and vessels," the act of twenty-second of February, eighteen hundred and forty-seven, entitled, "An act to regulate the carriage of passengers in merchant-vessels," the act of second March, eighteen hundred and forty-seven, entitled, "An act to amend an act entitled, 'An act to regulate the carriage of passengers in merchant vessels,' and to determine the time when said act shall take effect," the act of thirty-first January, eighteen hundred and forty-eight, entitled, "An act exempting vessels employed by the American Colonization Society in transporting colored emigrants from the United States to the coast of Africa from the provisions of the acts of the twenty-second February and second of March, eighteen hundred and forty-seven, regulating the carriage of passengers in merchant-vessels," the act of seventeenth May, eighteen hundred and forty-eight, entitled, "An act to provide for the ventilation of passenger-vessels, and for other purposes," and the act of third March, eighteen hundred and forty-nine, entitled, "An act to extend the provisions of all laws now in force relating to the carriage of passengers in merchant-vessels, and the regulations thereof," are hereby repealed. But nothing in this act contained shall in any wise obstruct or prevent the prosecution, recovery, distribution, or remission of any fines, penalties, or forfeitures, which may have been incurred in respect to any vessels prior to the day this act goes into effect, in respect to such vessels, under the laws hereby repealed, for which purpose the said laws shall continue in force.

But the Secretary of the Treasury may, in his discretion, and upon such conditions as he shall think proper, discontinue any such prosecutions, or remit or modify such penalties.

Approved, March 3, 1855.

General Regulations No. 45.—Under the act to regulate the carriage of passengers in steamships and other vessels, approved March 3, 1855.

To Collectors and other Officers of the Customs.

TREASURY DEPARTMENT, *March* 23, 1855.

THE attention of collectors and other officers of the customs, as well as all persons interested and engaged in carrying passengers in steamships and other vessels, is especially called to the provisions of the annexed act of Congress, approved March 3, 1855, entitled, "An act to regulate the carriage of passengers in steamships and other vessels," and a strict compliance with its terms and provisions enjoined upon the aforesaid officers and other persons interested.

It will be observed that, while this act prescribes spaces of certain clear superficial feet of deck to each passenger (other that cabin passengers), it moreover fixes a maximum by restricting the number of such passengers allowed to be carried in any such vessel in the proportion of one to every two tons of said vessel's tonnage measurement, excluding children under the age of one year from the computation, and computing two children over one and under eight years of age as one passenger. It follows, that though a vessel might afford clear spaces of the dimensions indicated for a greater number of passengers than one to every two tons of her tonnage measurement, yet if the number shall exceed that allowed by her tonnage measurement, the penalties imposed by the law would attach; or if her tonnage measurement should allow a greater number of passengers than according to the clear spaces prescribed by law she could carry, yet if the number shall exceed that allowed by the clear spaces prescribed by law, the penalties imposed by the law would equally attach. In other words, the one rule, as to the number of passengers a vessel is entitled to carry, is a limitation upon the other. The tonnage of each vessel, according to custom-house measurement, must, therefore, be ascertained, as well as the measurement of the spaces allotted to passengers, in order to determine the number of passengers she is entitled to carry.

In order to determine the number of passengers a vessel is entitled to carry in accordance with the spaces prescribed by this act, the height between decks must be measured from the bottom edge of the carlings or deck beams to the top floor below; and no space shall be considered available for passengers that has not, when measured in this manner, the height called for by the law, as the case may be; nor shall any space in a vessel of a less width than four feet be measured; provided, however, if the vessel shall, in accordance with the provisions of the first section of this act, carry any portion of her cargo, or any other article or articles, on any of the decks, cabins, or other places appropriated to the use of passengers, in lockers or enclosures prepared for the purpose, the height between decks shall be measured from the bottom edge of the carlings or deck beams to the upper surface of said lockers or enclosed spaces, which shall be deemed and taken to be the deck or platform from which measurement shall be made for all the purposes of this act, and the spaces occupied by said lockers or enclosed spaces shall be deducted from the spaces allowable for the use of passengers.

For example: the spaces in the main and poop decks or platforms, and in the deck-houses, if any there be, will be 16 by 6=96 feet; lower deck, 18 by 6=108 feet; two-deck vessels, 14 by 7½=105 feet.

The encumbering by merchandise or stores, not the personal baggage of the passengers, except in locker or enclosures prepared for the purpose, of any part of the space occupied by the passengers, will vitiate the whole space, unless the part so encumbered be separated from that so occupied, by a substantial bulkhead.

The deck or platform must be of a permanent nature, flush, and impervious to water.

Collectors will keep a special account of the moneys received under the fourteenth section of this act on account of deceased passengers; and, before making payments to any board or commission of the description mentioned in the law, will make a report to the Department of the number and designation of the boards or commissions appointed and acting under the authority of the State in which their respective ports are situated, to enable the Department to determine which is entitled to receive the same.

It will be perceived that the nineteenth section of this act expressly repeals all former laws on the subject, except so far as concerns the prosecution, recovery, distribution, or remission of any fines, penalties, and forfeitures which may have been incurred under former laws prior to the day this act shall go into effect; which, with respect to vessels sailing from ports in the United States on the eastern side of the continent, is within thirty days from the time of its approval; with respect to vessels sailing from ports in the United States on the western side of the continent, and from ports in Europe, is within sixty days from the time of its approval; and in respect to vessels sailing from ports in other parts of the world, is within six months from the time of its approval. The provisions of existing laws will be enforced until this act shall go into effect, as above specified.

It is deemed sufficient only further to call your particular attention to the first, second, sixth, tenth, eleventh, fourteenth, fifteenth, sixteenth, and seventeenth sections of this act, in which certain provisions, different from existing laws, have been enacted, and to state that all the requirements of said sections must be strictly enforced.

Collectors are directed to furnish the masters of all vessels engaged in transporting passengers between their respective ports and foreign countries, and each owner or consignee of any such vessel residing at their ports, with one copy of this circular.

JAMES GUTHRIE,
Secretary of the Treasury.

THE END.

www.ingramcontent.com/pod-product-compliance
Lightning Source LLC
LaVergne TN
LVHW011207110826
845150LV00006B/1344

* 9 7 8 1 4 2 5 5 1 8 4 8 6 *